Life Lessons
&
Selah Moments

A JOURNEY THROUGH THE STORY OF JOSHUA

Michelle M. Woodruff

NEWMAN SPRINGS PUBLISHING
320 Broad Street
Red Bank, NJ 07701

First originally published by Newman Springs Publishing 2020

ISBN 978-1-64801-991-3 (Paperback)
ISBN 978-1-64801-992-0 (Digital)

Printed in the United States of America

To my heavenly Father,
who truly is the Author and Finisher of this message.
Thank you for allowing me to be the pen in your hand
and the microphone through which you speak.

In Loving Memory

David Joseph Boudreau
May 3, 1955–July 16, 2020

I thought of you with love today, but that is nothing new.
I thought about you yesterday, and days before that too.
I think of you in silence, I often speak your name.
Now all I have is memories, and your pictures in a frame.
Your memory is my keepsake, with which I'll never part.
God has you in his keeping, I have you in my heart.
Love you, forever and always!

(author unknown)

Contents

Acknowledgments

It is with a grateful heart that I thank the following individuals who, without their encouragement and support, this book would not have been written.

Joey, Destiny, Jonny, Anissa, Jessica—my children, you are my greatest gifts! Thank you for your continual love, constant support, and never-ending encouragement. You are my joy and inspiration.

Maryanne Young, my sweet sister, thank you for all your uplifting encouragement and for the time you put into reading and critiquing this book. Your words of wisdom and insight are greatly appreciated.

Rabbi Cosmo Panzetta, thank you for imparting to me what God has imparted to you. Your faithfulness, integrity, and godly example of what true servant leadership is, is a highly treasured gift that myself and our congregation is truly blessed to have.

And last but by all means not least, a special thank you to my readers. May you take this life-changing message and go and change your world.

Foreword

Unprecedented—it's a word we hear used a lot these days. *The challenges we are facing are unprecedented. The tensions we are experiencing are unprecedented.* And on and on it goes. Maybe it's unprecedented. Maybe not. But in our day, we are experiencing things that *feel* unprecedented—"without previous instance; never before known or experienced; unexampled or unparalleled." And the challenge we experience in facing something that is (or seems to be) unprecedented is that we are left with the deer-in-the-headlights feeling of "I don't know what to do." We can't find a *precedent*, a previous occurrence of a similar circumstance that we can look upon and draw from in order to answer the question "how do we respond to what we're facing?"

When we are in search of a precedent, what we are basically in search of is a *lesson from the past.* We are in search of instruction for the present, practical, life-giving instruction. The Hebrew word for instruction is *Torah,* and the root word for Torah is *Or,* "light." "Your word is a lamp to my feet and a light to my path" (Psalm 119:105). When I'm facing what I've never faced, what do I do? Where do I look to find what I am to do? When I'm walking into the darkness of the unknown—into the darkness of the unprecedented—your Word, *ADONAI,* your Instruction, is what lights up the path. Your Word will guide me when I'm walking into the unknown, into what *feels* unprecedented.

This is all new to me…I don't know what to do.

It's new.

To ME.

But it isn't new to the sun (Ecclesiastes 1:9).

And it certainly isn't new to the One who formed the sun.

In the first chapter of the book of *Kohelet* ("The Preacher"), more widely known as the book of Ecclesiastes, the preacher says this:

> What has been is what will be, and what has been done will be done again. There is nothing new under the sun. Is there anything about which is said, "Look! This is new!"? It was already here long ago, in the ages long before us. There is no remembrance for former things, and things yet to come will not be remembered by those who follow. (Kohelet/Ecclesiastes 1:9–11)

Did you catch that? People are saying, "This is new! This is unprecedented!" But it's not new. While the specifics maybe new, the underlying principles are not. This has been going on for ages. It's just that in the moment of what *feels* unprecedented, most people are not actually remembering (calling to mind) the lessons from ages before us in order to draw wisdom—to gain lessons for today. Today, we are not learning the lessons from yesterday…and tomorrow, that cycle will be repeated. And those who follow us won't learn from the lessons of today. This isn't something the preacher is prophesying. It's a cycle that he is lamenting, a hamster wheel going nowhere.

But there's a way off the hamster wheel. Fear God. Keep his commands (Kohelet/Ecclesiastes 12:13). Look to the Lord! Let his Word—his instruction, his light—shine direction onto the darkened path before you. Call to mind what he has done!

And that's what Michelle has done in the book you are about to read, serving up profound life lessons with a beautiful simplicity as she looks back at life's journey through the book of Joshua to draw precedents and principles for our journey today. The details of today's journey may be new, but the principles are not.

One of the beautiful things about the long narrative portions of Scripture books like Joshua is that they convey to us the journey of real people who were walking with God without sanitizing the story in order to make them look better or perfect. Why mention that Rahab was a prostitute? Couldn't the writers have left that detail out? Why not just skip over the story of Achan's sin? That one is frustrating and embarrassing. Why not tweak the story of the Gibeonite deception? That just makes us look bad! But no. We are given access to the ups and the downs of the journey into the land that God had promised so that we can remember—call to mind—their journey with God. We get to see the real story so we can draw real-life lessons from their success *and* their failures.

You think what you're facing is unprecedented? Imagine what Joshua felt. As you embark on this journey through the book of Joshua, don't rush. Slow down. Pay attention. Don't assume that just because you've heard the story before that you already know and understand the lesson God has for you. As Michelle continually reminds us through this journey, *stop, look, listen.*

Let's look back to see how Joshua and Rahab and the children of Israel faced their unprecedented challenges so that we can look forward to face our unprecedented futures!

Rabbi Cosmo Panzetta
Lead Pastor, House of New Beginnings

What If...

Have you ever looked back on a situation in your life and wished you could have a do-over? Or perhaps you have reminisced about a time when you wished you had done things differently. Have you ever been bombarded by the all-too-familiar catch phrase "If only"? If only I knew then what I know now, things would be so different. If only I hadn't said that or if I hadn't traveled that path or made that choice—the should'ves, would'ves, and "if onlys" oftentimes become the catalyst for life lessons learned.

These life lessons provide powerful pieces of wisdom, knowledge, and insight that have been instrumental in improving one's self, one's relationships and, if truth be told, one's life in general. They are sanctified experiences that have helped shape us into who we have become today. Looking back on those experiences, we find that our takeaways have become valuable life lessons that we have gleaned along the way. The more life you experience, the more lessons you accumulate. The more lessons you learn, the more scars you will have to show for it.

But what if there was another way? What if you could actually learn a life lesson through the sanctified experiences of another? What if you could stand on the peripheral sidelines of someone else's life, seeing their life's story, and acquire those life lessons through the choices they've made and the paths they've taken?

What if those powerful pieces of wisdom, knowledge, and insight could be imparted to us through the life stories of those who have gone before us, thus, eliminating the unnecessary heartache caused by bad decisions and wrong choices? How sweet would that be? Just think about it—to be able to obtain wisdom through someone else's sanctified experiences. We would be given the ability to gain insight through someone else's story, benefiting from their life's journey minus the scars and heartache.

But that would require something from us. It would require a commitment to follow alongside, intently listening and quietly observing, looking beyond the obvious to that which is hidden for those truly seeking.

Will you follow? Will you have eyes that see? Will you have ears that listen? Will you have a heart that is willing to change? Therein lies the crux of the matter.

You see, we are quick to say we will follow. Our desire is to both see and hear. However, with some of us, when it comes to change, there is a slight shift in our stance, a subtle hesitation that can be detected as we verbally or mentally ask the following questions:

"Change?"

"What do you mean by change?"

"Why do I need to change?"

Then there are those of us who want change. We need change, and we know it. For those of us in that group, the very thought of change excites us. That is, until we are pushed out of our comfort zone into the world of the unknown. When change begins to take place in our lives, and we start to experience a transition into something we may have never experienced before, we oftentimes have the tendency to put on the brakes.

"Wait a minute. This is different."

"This doesn't feel right."

"I've never done it this way before."

"I'm not too comfortable with this new way of doing things."

Change—it is a two-sided coin. We cling to the hope that God has promised us a new beginning, a fresh start, if you would. After all, Scripture encourages us to forget the old and to embrace newness of life.

> Do not remember the former things, nor consider things of the past. Here I am, doing a new thing; Now it is springing up—do you not know about it? I will surely make a way in the desert, rivers in the wasteland. (Isaiah 43:18–19)

With this hope for change, there comes a sense of excitement about new beginnings, and then the coin flips. As soon as that change comes and the transition to newness of life begins, fear and hesitation step in.

Change forces us out of the comfortable and into the unknown. After all, it's a new beginning, filled with new experiences. We don't know what to expect as we have never traveled this way before. We are both excited and hesitant as we enter into this unknown territory. What we all need is a push in the right direction, a slight shove that enables us to bypass our hesitancy, allowing us to step right into what God has for us.

I'm reminded of a story that took place back in the mid-1800s. There was a man who had a thought, and as he meditated on that thought, it began to take on a life of its own. The more he thought, the more it evolved, until finally, his thought became reality.

The man's name was Elisha Graves Otis, and more often than not, you will see his name imprinted on the *elevator* that you are riding.

Now a few years after Otis's invention, there was an elderly couple who made a trip into the big city. They lived in the country and could really only make this trip once or twice every few years. Now the husband had heard about Otis's contraption, never seen it but had heard that it would change your world as you know it.

So he and his wife arrived in the city and checked into their hotel. The wife wanted to use the facilities, so the husband said he would wait for her by Otis's elevator. The man went and found the elevator and just stood in front of it, staring at it. A few seconds went by, and another lady came over, about the same age as his wife. She went up to the elevator, looked at the buttons on the side, chose one, and pushed it. The doors disappeared. Well, this got the old man's attention. She stepped in, and the doors reappeared.

By this time, his wife had come and was standing by his side. Moments later, the elevator doors disappeared again, and out walked a young beautiful blonde. The guy's mouth dropped open as this young lady stepped out of Otis's elevator. He quickly grabbed his wife and shoved her in. If change were only that easy, right?

As followers and disciples of *Yeshua* Messiah, it is our responsibility to surrender to the process that will bring about the necessary changes in our lives. Now, as we know, change can be both instantaneous as well as progressive.

Here, from Paul's written words to the believers in Corinth, we learn that for those of us who have received God's *salvation*, an instantaneous change takes place.

> Therefore, if anyone is in Messiah [*Christ*], he is a new creation. The old things have passed away; behold, all things have become new. (2 Corinthians 5:17)

It is in Yeshua that we become the *righteousness* of God; we are made holy even as he is holy. It is now our responsibility to maintain that holiness so that we can carry out the directive (the why behind the what) we see written here in Paul's letter to the believers in Rome.

> I urge you therefore, brothers and sisters, by the mercies of God to present your bodies as a living sacrifice—holy, acceptable to God—which is your spiritual service. Do not be conformed to this world but be transformed by the renewing of your mind, so that you may discern what is the will of God—what is good and acceptable and perfect. (Romans 12:1–2)

As believers in Messiah Yeshua, our spiritual service is to present our bodies as a living sacrifice, a sacrifice that is both holy and acceptable. Some Bible translations even say that this is our reasonable service—in other words, this isn't an unreasonable request of God. It's an expectation of God. He has made us holy, and he expects us to maintain that holiness.

The only way you and I can do this is if we apply the truths laid out for us in this passage. If we are to present ourselves as holy and acceptable to God, we cannot conform to this world's way of thinking, acting, or speaking. We cannot imitate the world's behavioral patterns or thought patterns and be pleasing and acceptable to God.

The only way we will not conform to this world's way of thinking, doing, and speaking is if we are transformed from the inside out. There has to be an inner change that takes place. This is where the progressive part of salvation comes into play.

When we received Yeshua as our Lord and Savior, we were instantly changed from darkness into light. However, there is a daily dying to self that is required, an inner transformation that God so desires to take place on the inside of us, thus, resulting in us becoming a clearer representation of the image we were originally created in.

Change—it is as inevitable as it is necessary. If only it were as easy as stepping onto an elevator and leaving it as a changed man or woman. But as we all know, that's not how life works.

On the other hand, life does offer us experiences that can bring about life lessons, lessons that if applied to our lives on a daily basis will become the very instrument that allow us to undergo that inner transformation, an inner transformation that God so desires in each and every one of our lives.

How very blessed you and I are to live in a day and age where we can look back through history and glean the life lessons God has taught his people as they learned how to follow, how to see, how to hear, and how to change. What if we could learn these lessons through the examples set before us?

The answer to that question is, we can. You see, God has so graciously given us living examples, all throughout Scripture, of men and women who have gone on before us, people just like you and I whose life stories are full of lessons learned throughout their journey. One such example is Joshua.

As some of you may know, the Hebrew name for Joshua is *Y'hoshua* (Ya-hoe-shoe-a), which means "ADONAI is salvation." An alternative form of the name *Y'hoshua* is Yeshua which, of course, when translated into English is Jesus. Joshua, chosen by God, was an instrument of ADONAI's salvation that led the children of Israel out of the wilderness into the Land of Promise.

So I invite you to walk with me as we follow Joshua on a journey that will be familiar and yet quite different, a walk through Scripture that will allow you to see passages from different vantage points, thus, enabling you to gain perhaps a newer and deeper perspective.

Through this journey, we will glean various life lessons as we take an in-depth look at the sanctified experiences throughout the leadership of Joshua. Through these experiences, we will not only learn the life lessons of Joshua, but we will learn how to apply those same lessons to our lives on a daily basis. In the process, we will also learn what it means to take a *selah moment*. Push the pause button. Stop. Look. Listen. You see, a selah moment is a process of stopping what we are doing, looking toward our Savior, and listening to his voice and only his voice.

However, that's not the end of the journey. You see, it's not enough to simply learn these Life Lessons or to take these selah moments. The secret is the application of those truths in our personal lives. Yet even in that, there is still more to do. As believers in Messiah Yeshua, we have been tasked with the responsibility of taking that which has been imparted to us and sharing those truths with others.

Paul speaks of this very thing in his letter to the believers in Rome when he writes of imparting to them what God had so freely given to him.

> For I am yearning to see you, that I may impart and share with you some spiritual gift to strengthen and establish you. (Romans 1:11 AMPC)

We are to be disciples who make disciples who make disciples. It is taking this mandate from Yeshua seriously and owning it.

> Go therefore and make disciples of all nations, immersing them in the name of the Father and the Son and the Ruach ha-Kodesh [*Holy Spirit*], teaching them to observe all I have commanded you. And remember! I am with you always, even to the end of the age. (Matthew 28:19–20)

Every one of you reading these words will glean something unique from these life lessons, truths seen through the personal lens of your life. As you adopt these truths and apply them to your life, you will then be able to share these powerful pieces of wisdom, knowledge, and insight with those who make up your world.

> For whatever was written before was written for our instruction, so that through patience and the encouragement of the Scriptures we might have hope. (Romans 15:4)

So let the journey begin!

Joshua, the Man

The book of Joshua is oftentimes referred to as a book of remembrance. It was written as a reminder to the people of Israel that deliverance comes through God and him alone, a constant reminder that victory comes only through trusting him and obeying his commands. However, it is also a reminder that defeat, ruin, and disgrace come through disobedience and an absence of faith.

Though the book of Joshua begins in the year 1400 BCE, his story began earlier than that. So just who is Joshua, the man?

We first learn of this young man during the children of Israel's journey through the wilderness. It is here where we have our first glimpse into his character, a character that reveals him as a man of action.

An enemy army had come against Israel, and Moses chose Joshua to lead Israel's soldiers against the soldiers of Amalek.

> Then the Amalekites came and fought with Israel at Rephidim. Moses said to Joshua, 'Choose men, go out, and fight the Amalekites. Tomorrow I will stand on the top of the hill with the staff of God in my hand.' So, Joshua did as Moses said, and fought the Amalekites, while Moses, Aaron and Hur went up to the top of the hill. (Exodus 17:8–10)

The Amalekites had come out against Israel, declaring war upon them. Joshua, chosen by Moses, had become the leader and commander of Israel's army. Taking his men, Joshua went down into the valley of Rephidim where he engaged in face-to-face combat with the enemy.

Meanwhile, Moses went and stood upon the hilltop overlooking this battlefield. His job was to extend the rod of God up over that battlefield. As you probably know, this was no ordinary staff. It was a representation not only of God's presence but of his power and authority as well.

As long as the staff of God was raised high above the battlefield, the Israelites prevailed. But as the battle waged on, Moses began to feel the weight of this fight. With arms heavy, inadvertently, Moses's arms began to lower as weariness set in. With the lowering of his arms, the battle quickly turned against the Israelites, and the Amalekites now prevailed.

Recognizing what was happening, Aaron and Hur came alongside of Moses and led him to a rock where he could rest. Together, they lifted up his hands over that battlefield and proclaimed God's presence, power, and authority over that enemy. Israel prevailed. The battle was won. The enemy defeated.

> So, Joshua overpowered the Amalekites and his army with the edge of the sword. ADONAI said to Moses, "Write this for a memorial in the book, and rehearse it in the hearing for Joshua, for I will utterly blot out the memory of the Amalekites from under heaven." Then Moses built an altar, and called the name of it, ADONAI-Nissi. (Exodus 17:13–15)

There is a particular word that I want to draw your attention to in this passage, and that is the word *rehearse*. Now when we think of this word, we think of practicing something over and over and over again. However, the Hebrew definition of this word means much more than that.

Rehearse—this word is derived from the Hebrew word *suwm*, which means "to put into, place into or set in place."[1] In essence, it means to get it inside of you. It was at this place that ADONAI revealed himself as *ADONAI-Nissi*—the Lord is my banner.

ADONAI was their banner of protection. He was their covering. Moses was commanded by God to rehearse the happenings of this divine intervention in the ears of Joshua day after day after day until faith built up in him.

Moses was to put into the spirit of Joshua this truth of God. He is our covering. He is our protection. It wasn't the agility of Joshua or his cunning stratagems that brought about Israel's victory. It was God himself. He was their banner. He was their protection. This was a truth that Moses was instructed to set in place so that (again, the why behind the what) Joshua's trust in God would be built up.

> So, faith comes from hearing and hearing by the
> word of Messiah. (Romans 10:17)

As Moses rehearsed this in the ears of Joshua, faith was growing in him. A simple trust and an absolute confidence in God were being built up in Joshua every time Moses repeated this victory in his hearing.

The next major encounter with Joshua is approximately two years later. Through this encounter with him, we see him as a man of faith.

Once again, he is chosen by Moses, along with eleven other men, to go on a covert mission across the Jordan. Twelve spies, a leader from each of their tribes, were sent over the Jordan to the Promised Land. Their mission was to spy out the land and to bring back a report to Moses and the children of Israel.

For forty days, they traveled in secrecy, spying out the land God had given to them. It was incredible; it truly was a land flowing with milk and honey. Joshua and the other spies even cut some of its fruit to bring back and show the people. They would be amazed; just one single branch with a cluster of grapes took two of their strongest to carry it on a pole between them.

These men had traveled together, explored together, and worked together. They saw everything that this land offered together. Yet, upon their return, the report given by ten of their team members was filled with fear because of the sons of Anak and Amalek who were living in the land.

Wait a minute. What? They had already defeated the Amalekites once before, and Joshua knew this. He, along with Caleb, told the people that they could, with certainty, defeat them. Didn't they remember? God did it once before. He could do it again.

> Then Caleb quieted the people before Moses, and said, "We should definitely go up and capture the land, for we can certainly do it!" (Numbers 13:30)

> Joshua son of Nun and Caleb son of Jephunneh, who were among those who had explored the land, tore their clothes. They said to the whole assembly of Bnei-Yisrael [*children of Israel*], "The land through which we passed is an exceptionally good land! If ADONAI is pleased with us, He will lead us into that land and will give it to us—a land flowing with milk and honey. Only don't rebel against ADONAI, and don't be afraid of the people of the land. They will be food for us. The protection over them is gone. ADONAI is with us! Do not fear them." (Numbers 14:6–9)

Another occasion where we are given a small glimpse into the character of Joshua was at Mt. Sinai. Here in this passage, we see Joshua as a man of perseverance and tenacity.

The Ten Words of God, or the Ten Commandments, had just been spoken to the people. Moses had been instructed by God to bring Aaron, Nadab, and Abihu along with the seventy elders of Israel and come to the base of the mountain. There they were to worship the God of Abraham, Isaac, and Jacob.

> Then Moses and Aaron, Nadab and Abihu, and seventy of the elders of Israel went up. They saw the God of Israel, and under His feet was something like a pavement of sapphire, as clear as the very heavens. Yet He did not raise His hand

against the nobles of Bnei-Yisrael [*children of Israel*]. So, they beheld God, and ate and drank. Then ADONAI said to Moses, "Come up to Me on the mountain and stay there, and I will give the tablets of stone with the Torah and the mitzvot [*commandments*], which I have written so that you may instruct them." So, Moses rose up along with his attendant Joshua, and Moses went up on the mountain of God. Exodus 24:9–12)

When Moses came down from that mountain, after being up there for forty days and forty nights, Joshua was still waiting for him at the same place Moses left him. He never left, which means Joshua was at the foot of that mountain for forty days and forty nights as well.

Then Moses turned and went down from the mountain, with the two tablets of the Testimony in his hand, tablets that were written on both sides, on one and on the other. The tablets were the work of God, and the writing was the writing of God, engraved on the tablets. When Joshua heard the noise of the people as they shouted, he said to Moses, "There is the sound of war within the camp." (Exodus 32:15–17)

We then read of Joshua staying at the Tent of Meeting long after Moses had departed. This was the meeting place of God. Everyone who sought ADONAI would go out to the Tent of Meeting which was located just outside the camp. It is here where we see Joshua as a man of prayer.

So, ADONAI spoke with Moses face to face, as a man speaks with his friend. Then he would return to the camp, but his servant Joshua, the son of Nun, a young man, did not leave the tent. (Exodus 33:11)

Throughout Exodus and the children of Israel's journey through the wilderness, we have caught small glimpses into the character of Joshua. Just prior to his death, Moses further validates Joshua and the call of God upon his life.

> Then Moses summoned Joshua and said to him in the sight of all Israel, "Be strong! Be courageous! For you are to go with this people into the land ADONAI has sworn to their fathers to give them, and you are to enable them to inherit it. ADONAI—He is the One who goes before you. He will be with you. He will not fail you or abandon you. Do not fear or be discouraged. (Deuteronomy 31:7–8)

So who was Joshua, the *man*? He was a man of action, faith, and perseverance. Joshua was a man of prayer, and he was the man chosen by God to lead his people.

New Beginnings

The book of Joshua opens with a new day dawning for Israel. Moses had died and the thirty-day mourning period had passed. It was the end of an era and the beginning of a new chapter in the lives of the Israelites. Up until this point in their wilderness journey, the only leadership the children of Israel ever experienced was that of Moses. But that's all about to change. Joshua was now the new leader of Israel, chosen by God, to lead his people into the Promised Land.

> Now it came about after the death of Moses the servant of ADONAI that ADONAI spoke to Joshua son of Nun, Moses' aide saying: "My servant Moses is dead. So now, arise, you and all these people, cross over this Jordan to the land that I am giving to them—to Bnei-Yisrael [(children of Israel.)] (Joshua 1:1–2)

At this point in our story, the Israelites were still camped east of the Jordan, though their focus was aimed toward Canaan and Israel's future there. The children of God were poised to enter the land long promised to them. Their assignment was to take the land by force. According to rumor, the inhabitants of the land were gigantic, fierce, and ready to fight to defend their turf.

It had been a long time coming, but finally, God had given the command to cross over. However, their beloved leader, Moses, had died. Unlike their parents, they didn't have an enraged army chasing after them. What they did have though was a leadership change. Joshua, the servant of Moses, had now become their leader.

They had grown up with Joshua. They had heard the story depicting him as a man of action as he led the army in battle against the Amalekites. Some of them, as children, would have seen him as a man of faith who stood alongside Caleb as they pleaded with their fathers to trust God and take the land forty years earlier.

I'm sure they had heard the stories of his perseverance and faithfulness in prayer at the foot of the mountain and at the Tent of Meeting. But could he honestly fill the shoes of Moses? Could he ever come close to the type of leader Moses was?

Indeed, change had come, and on the heels of that change, a transition was about to take place. Change. Transitions. New beginnings. This brings us to the first Life Lesson we can glean from Joshua: *with each and every change, there is always a promise and a word of instruction.*

A leadership change had taken place. The mantle of authority had been passed down from Moses to Joshua. God declared it. Moses validated it. Joshua received it. Now comes the promise.

> Every place on which the sole of your foot treads, I am giving to you, as I spoke to Moses. From the wilderness and this Lebanon to the great river, the Euphrates River—all the land of the Hittites—to the Great Sea toward the setting of the sun will be your territory. No one will be able to stand before you all the days of your life. Just as I was with Moses, so I will be with you. I will not fail you or forsake you. (Joshua 1:3–5)

Here within this passage, we see a threefold promise, a promise of possession, protection, and presence. With the promise of possession, God declared that he was giving them the land. With the promise of protection, God proclaimed that no one would be able to stand before them. Last but not least, with the promise of his presence, God decreed, "I am with you."

Immediately following this threefold promise, God provided a word of instruction to Joshua.

> Chazak! Be strong! For you will lead these peo-
> ple to inherit the land I swore to their fathers to
> give them. Only be very strong, and resolute to
> observe diligently the Torah which Moses, My
> servant commanded you. Do not turn from it to
> the right or to the left, so you may be successful
> where you go. This book of the Torah should not
> depart from your mouth—you are to meditate
> on it day and night, so that you may be careful
> to do everything written in it. For then you will
> make your ways prosperous and then you will be
> successful. Have I not commanded you? Chazak!
> Be strong! Do not be terrified or dismayed, for
> ADONAI your God is with you wherever you go.
> (Joshua 1:6–9)

The very words that Moses spoke to Joshua prior to his death were repeated here but were now coming directly from the mouth of God. The Hebrew word *chazak* used in this passage means "to be strong, to become strong and to grow in strength."[2]

God was instructing Joshua to take courage and to remember who God is. He was to draw his strength and courage from God and God alone, for therein lay his strength.

In and of himself, Joshua did not have the type of strength necessary to lead the children of Israel. Nor did he have the power within himself to defeat the enemies of the land.

Nor do you and I. In and of ourselves, we don't have the type of strength needed to face off and defeat the enemy. However, when we call out to God in our weakness, there is an unleashing of power that takes place. This unleashing of God's power from the inside of us overshadows our weakness with his strength.

The apostle Paul speaks of this unleashing of God's power in his letter to the believers in Corinth.

> But He said to me, "My grace is sufficient for you, for power is made perfect in weakness." Therefore, I boast all the more gladly in my weaknesses, so that the power of Messiah may dwell in me. (2 Corinthians 12:9)

As God was giving his word of instruction to Joshua, he didn't just tell Joshua to be strong and courageous. He actually revealed to him how and where that strength could be drawn from.

> Only be very strong, and resolute to observe diligently the Torah which Moses, My servant commanded you. Do not turn from it to the right or to the left, so you may be successful where you go. (Joshua 1:7)

There are two words in particular that I want to draw your attention to in this verse. The first word is *resolute*. This word means to be "firm in purpose, determined, and unwavering."[3]

The second word in this verse is *observe*. This word means to "keep, guard, retain, treasure and protect."[4]

We are to be firm in purpose, determined, and unwavering when it comes to keeping God's word, guarding his word, and retaining his word. We are also to be firm in purpose, determined and unwavering when it comes to treasuring and protecting God's word. The psalmist writes about this very thing in Psalm chapter 119.

> How can a young man keep his way pure? By guarding it according to Your word. With my whole heart have I sought You—let me not stray from Your mitzvot [*commandments*]. I have treasured Your word in my heart, so I might not sin against You. (Psalm 119:9–11)

God's instruction to Joshua was to diligently treasure God's word, to keep it and to guard it, fully retaining all that it says. This takes strength, discipline, and commitment.

This is a daily process that God has instituted for us to remain connected and instructed. It is through his word that we gain insight, and it is through his word that we become strong.

We see here an intentionality associated with this command. Again, God told Joshua to be resolute in following Torah. It is a firm purpose, with a determination that is unwavering.

I will not be distracted. I will not veer off to the left or the right. I will fix my eyes upon God's truth, and I will maintain my focus upon God.

The writer of Hebrews speaks of this very thing when he tells us to look away from all that distracts and to fix our focus on Yeshua who is our salvation.

> Therefore, since we have such a great cloud of witnesses surrounding us, let us also get rid of every weight and entangling sin. Let us run with endurance the race set before us, focusing on Yeshua, the initiator and perfecter of faith. For the joy set before Him, He endured the cross, disregarding its shame and He has taken His seat at the right hand of the throne of God. Consider Him who has endured such hostility by sinners against himself, so that you may not grow weary in your souls and lose heart. (Hebrews 12:1–3)

Joshua's success, the success of the children of Israel, and our success is all contingent upon hearing and doing.

> This book of the Torah should not depart from your mouth—you are to meditate on it day and night, so that you may be careful to do every-thing written in it. For then you will make your

ways prosperous and then you will be successful.
(Joshua 1:8)

The first phrase I want to draw your attention to is the phrase
"day and night." This is a Hebrew expression that means *always*. First
Chronicles 16:11 reads, "Seek ADONAI and His strength, seek His
face always."

The second phrase that I want to bring to your attention is "so
that." This is a phrase that we see all throughout Scripture, and it
points to the why behind the what. Whenever you see this phrase,
take what I like to call a selah moment. Stop. Listen and see the *why*
behind the *what*.

God's instruction for us is to meditate upon his Torah, always
with the understanding that the Torah is more than just the instruction of God. It is the very heart of God. It is within the Torah that
God's character, his very nature is revealed to us. It is his Word, and
it is to never depart from our mouth.

Just as God told Moses to rehearse these words to Joshua, we are
to rehearse the righteous rulings of our God day and night, night and
day. We see this truth reiterated for us in the book of Psalms.

> I have treasured Your word in my heart, so I might
> not sin against You. Blessed are You, ADONAI.
> Teach me Your statues. With my lips I rehearse
> all the rulings of Your mouth. (Psalm 119:11–13)

In one of the psalms that King David wrote, he declares that
God's Torah is a Tree of Wisdom to those who delight in it.

> Happy is the one who has not walked in the
> advice of the wicked, nor stood in the way of sin-
> ners, nor sat in the seat of scoffers. But his delight
> is in the Torah of ADONAI, and on His Torah, he
> meditates day and night. He will be like a planted
> tree over streams of water, producing its fruit

during its season. Its leaf never droops—but in all he does, he succeeds. (Psalm 1:1–3)

We are to mediate on the Torah, God's Word, day and night so that—again, the *why* behind the *what*—we may be careful to do everything that is written in it.

In his last sermon, Moses told the children of Israel exactly what God expected and required of them.

> So now, O Israel, what does ADONAI your God require of you, but to fear ADONAI your God, to walk in all His ways and love Him, and to serve ADONAI your God with all your heart and with all your soul, to keep the mitzvot [*commandments*] of ADONAI and His statues that I am commanding you today, for your own good. (Deuteronomy 10:12–13)

The word that I want to draw to your attention in this passage comes from the Hebrew word *yare* which has been translated into the English word *fear*. This word means to "revere, honor and respect, to stand in awe of and to have a godly fear."[5]

Within this passage, Moses tells us exactly what God expects from us as his children. We are to:

- Revere, honor and respect him,
- Stand in awe of him,
- Walk in his ways,
- Love and serve him,
- Keep his commands,
- Uphold his word.

By doing this, we will see the goodness of God flowing in and through our lives. We are again reminded of ADONAI's expectations through the words of the prophet Micah.

He has told you, humanity, what is good, and
what ADONAI is seeking from you: Only to prac-
tice justice, to love mercy, and to walk humbly
with your God. The voice of ADONAI calls to the
city—it is wisdom to fear Your Name—Pay attention to the rod and to the One who appointed it.
(Micah 6:8–9)

Referring back to Joshua 1:8, the word *meditate* is derived from
the Hebrew word *hagah*, and it means more than just focusing your
thoughts on something. It also means "to utter, to speak and to
rehearse that which you are focusing upon."[6]

We are to fix our mind on God's word, his Torah, and we are
to focus our thoughts on what he says, and then we are to repeat or
rehearse the righteous sayings of our God. We are to hear, we are to
do, and we are to speak.

Moses repeatedly spoke this truth to the children of Israel. We
see it again in the sixth chapter of Deuteronomy. As we read the
words of Moses, I want you to pay close attention to the phrase "so
that," and take a selah moment. Stop. Look. Listen. Take a moment
to see the why behind the what.

Now this is the commandment, the statutes and
ordinances that ADONAI your God commanded
to teach you to do in the land you are crossing
over to possess—*so that* you might fear ADONAI
your God, to keep all His statues and mitzvot
[*commandments*] that I am commanding you and
your son and your son's son all the days of your
life, and *so that* you may prolong your days. Hear,
therefore, O Israel, and take care to do this, *so
that* it may go well with you and you may increase
mightily, as ADONAI the God of your fathers has
promised you, in a land flowing with milk and
honey. "Hear O Israel, the Lord our God, the
Lord is one. Love ADONAI your God with all

your heart and with all your soul and all your strength. These words, which I am commanding you today, are to be on your heart. You are to teach them diligently to your children, and speak of them when you sit in your house, when you walk by the way, when you lie down and when you rise up. Bind them as a sign on your hand, they are to be as frontlets between your eyes, and write them on the doorposts of your house and on your gates. (Deuteronomy 6:1–9; emphasis mine)

Moses relayed to the children of Israel God's expectations, and in so doing, provided the why behind the what. This is what you are to do and why.

- So that...
  - o You might *fear* ADONAI
  - o You may prosper
- So that...
  - o It may go well with you
  - o You may increase mightily

Immediately following this instruction, God spoke through Moses and issued a warning to the children of Israel. The warning was simply this, do not forget God.

Then watch yourself so that you do not forget ADONAI who brought you from the land of Egypt, from the house of slavery. (Deuteronomy 6:12)

Unfortunately, we know from Scripture that was exactly what the children of Israel did.

Thus, says ADONAI: "What fault did your fathers find in Me that they strayed so far from Me?

They walked after worthless things, becoming worthless themselves?" (Jeremiah 2:5)

"Has a nation changed its gods—even though they are not gods? Yet My people have exchanged their glory for worthless things. Be appalled at this, O heavens! Be utterly horrified and dumbfounded." It is a declaration of ADONAI. "My people have committed two evils: They have forsaken Me—the spring of living water—and they dug their own cisterns—cracked cisterns that hold no water." (Jeremiah 2:11–13)

"Your own wickedness will rebuke you and your backslidings will rebuke you. Know then and see how bad and bitter it is for you to forsake ADONAI your God. Nor is fear of Me in you." It is a declaration of the Lord ADONAI-Tzva'ot [*Lord God of hosts*]. (Jeremiah 2:19)

Can a virgin forget her ornaments, or a bride her attire? Yet My people have forgotten Me, days without number. (Jeremiah 2:32)

Can you imagine being forgotten days without number? Just think about it for a moment. Imagine not even being a passing thought in the mind of the one you love—completely forgotten, overlooked, disregarded. The sadness associated with those words is almost tangible. No one wants to feel that way. We've all heard the saying, "If those are my friends, who needs enemies." And yet, these are the emotions we have caused God to feel.

How very sad to think that after all God had done for the children of Israel, they simply forgot all about him. He didn't just slip their mind for a brief moment. Scripture says they went for days without even thinking of him.

How could anyone do that? What kind of people were these Israelites? If truth be told, they are the same kind of people you and I are.

How many times have we done this same thing? How many days have gone by with us not even opening up our Bibles?

Oh, we may have said a quick prayer here and there throughout our week and called it good. But when was the last time you had a full-blown conversation with God, a conversation that entailed listening and hearing what he had to say and not just a one-sided conversation that was only comprised of a to-do list for him?

Many of us are guilty of going from one Saturday morning or Sunday morning service without once getting into his Word in the in-between time.

Forgotten. Overlooked. Disregarded.

Now would be a good time to take a selah moment. Stop. Look. Listen. Pay close attention to what God is trying to show you. If the truth revealed here has resonated within your heart, own up to it. Ask God to truly forgive you, and may these words never again be associated with your relationship with him.

Moving forward, God had given Joshua a promise long before he experienced the change that promise was associated with. Along with that promise came a set of instructions, a word of direction that would enable him to transition into a new beginning.

Change was upon them. Transition was inevitable. However, blessings would be found on the other side of both. On the other side of this new beginning, Joshua and the children of Israel would need to face their enemies.

God had given them a promise, but they were going to need to draw their strength from him. They were going to need to be resolute in maintaining their focus. Yes, the battle was God's, but they were still going to be entering into enemy territory.

So they would need to be strong—very strong! They would need to diligently remain in the presence of God, obeying his every instruction so that they might succeed and prosper in their way.

New beginnings require both transition and change. During any season of change, it is imperative to fix our focus continually on

God. Listen for his voice and follow his direction. Never forget that with every change there is a threefold promise of possession, protection, and presence. Immediately on the heels of that promise will be God's word of instruction for you, enabling you to inherit your promised land.

God's Unexpected Answer

The time had finally come for the children of Israel to cross over the Jordan into the land that God had promised to give them. This was a land that God had told them they would need to take by force, a land whose inhabitants had been rumored to be gigantic, fierce, and ready to fight to defend what they believed to be theirs.

Yet interestingly enough, Joshua didn't instruct the children of Israel to prepare for battle. In light of what they were about to face, you think their focus would be on preparing their weapons for eminent war. Instead, we find them gathering food for their journey.

> Then Joshua commanded the officials of the people saying: "Go through the camp and charge the people saying: 'Prepare provisions, for within three days you will be crossing over this Jordan, to go in to possess the land which Adonai your God is giving you to possess it.'" (Joshua 1:10–11)

Once again, we see a subtle reminder that the battle belongs to the Lord, and it would be done his way and with his choice of weaponry. Joshua gave the command: Get ready! Prepare food for the journey, for in three days, we are crossing over the Jordan.

With the attention of the children of Israel focused on preparing provisions for their journey, Joshua pulled aside two of his most trusted men. His intention was to secretly send them on a covert mission. Their assignment was to spy out the land and bring back a report.

If you'll remember, forty years earlier, Joshua was part of an exploration team whose sole purpose was to spy out the land and bring back a good report to Moses. Twelve men were chosen—a leader from each tribe. They traveled together, explored together, and worked together as a team. Together, they saw everything the land had to offer.

Yet, when it came time to share their experiences with Moses and the children of Israel, ten of the twelve viewed this experience through the eyes of fear and uncertainty. These ten men described the inhabitants of the land as powerful and gigantic. The cities were fortified and impregnable.

The more they talked, the more their fear took over. The land was no longer described as a land filled with milk and honey but as a land that devoured its residents. In their eyes, these men saw themselves as grasshoppers in the land of giants.

I can just imagine the looks of utter astonishment on the faces of Joshua and Caleb as they were listening to their counterparts.

"Wait!"

"What?"

"That's not what we saw!"

"That's your takeaway?"

Joshua and Caleb saw through the eyes of faith and certainty, whereas these other men saw through the eyes of their own inabilities and inadequacies. Fear and doubt suddenly clashed with faith and certainty. Caleb and Joshua countered this evil report with these words of faith and certainty.

> Then Caleb quieted the people before Moses, and said, "We should definitely go up and capture the land, for we can certainly do it!" (Numbers 13:30)

Joshua and Caleb spoke out a second time the following day, trying to convince the people that God was with them, and he is greater than any foe they might face.

> They said to the whole assembly of Bnei-Yisrael [*children of Israel*], "The land through which we

passed is an exceptionally good land! If ADONAI
is pleased with us, He will lead us into that land
and will give it to us—a land flowing with milk
and honey. Only don't rebel against ADONAI, and
don't be afraid of the people of the land. They
will be food for us. The protection over them
is gone. ADONAI is with us! Do not fear them!
(Numbers 14:7–9)

Forty years had come and gone since that day. Those who chose
to distrust God and his character had since died in that wilderness.
Now a new day was dawning.

I believe it would be safe to surmise that Joshua was probably
remembering that experience and how everything played out. With
the events of that time so fresh within his memory, Joshua chose a
different means of exploration.

Through discernment, discretion, and divine direction he chose
two of his most trusted men. In the midst of activity, while everyone's attention was focused elsewhere, Joshua pulled them aside and
briefed them on the covert mission he had for them.

They were to slip away, making sure no one saw them. They
were to cross the Jordan and spy out the land—especially Jericho.
They were to return in three days with their report.

In that day and age, Jericho was the most important Canaanite
fortified city in the Jordan Valley. It was the principal seat of idol
worship, being especially devoted to *Ashtaroth*, the goddess of the
moon. Jericho was known for all that was the vilest and most degrad-
ing in the religion of the Canaanite, and that was their destination.
Jericho was their mission.

With the day coming to a close and night fast approaching, the
two spies set out. Leaving Shittim for Jericho, they covertly entered
the city and found lodging at the home of the prostitute Rahab.

Then Joshua son of Nun secretly sent out two
spies from Shittim saying: "Go, explore the land,
especially Jericho." So, they went and came to

the house of a prostitute whose name was Rahab, and lodged there. The king of Jericho was told, "Some men from Bnei-Yisrael have just come here tonight to spy out the land." So, the king of Jericho sent word to Rahab saying: "Bring out the men who came to you, who entered your house—for they have come to spy out all the land." (Joshua 2:1–3

If we are not careful, we could easily miss a hidden truth in that passage. You see, Israel wasn't the only one in the "spy business." There were also Canaanite spies keeping their eyes on *Bnei*-Yisrael, spies who were fully aware of the comings and goings of the Israelite people.

Shortly after the arrival of the Israeli spies, their presence was made known to the king of Jericho. He was informed of who they were and where they were staying. Their cover was blown. Their mission compromised. Immediately, the king sent a message to Rahab, telling her to bring out the men who came to her home, declaring to her in the missive that they were spies.

For just a moment, I want us to pause here and take a selah moment. Oftentimes, when we are reading or hearing a familiar passage, there is a tendency to breeze on through.

We know what it says. We've either read or heard it a hundred times over. It's in those moments of familiarity that we need to intentionally take a selah moment.

Stop. Look. Listen. Stop—think about what you've just read. Look—see the truths hidden beneath the surface. Listen—hear the still, small voice of God as he speaks.

These men from across the Jordan were the enemy. They were spies. Their mission was to spy out the land.

Just so we're clear on this, the definition of the word *spy* is "to watch secretly, usually for hostile purposes." It refers to a person who tries secretly to get information about a country for another country's purposes.[7]

This was a crime. The punishment upon capture would be certain death. If you were caught harboring a criminal of this nature, it would be considered an act of treason. An act that is also punishable by death.

> But the woman took the two men and hid them, and said: "Yes, the men did come to me, but I didn't know where they were from. So, when it was time to shut the gate at dark, the men went out, and I don't know where they went. Pursue them quickly, for you may overtake them." (Joshua 2:4–6)

Rahab risked everything—her life and her family's life—in order to spare these two men who have come from Israel's camp.

The thing we need to understand here is that when the king of Jericho sent word to Rahab about these men, it wasn't simply a letter being dropped off in the mail. Nor was it a message sent by courier that upon delivery, the messenger's duty was done. No! This message from the king was personally delivered by his soldiers. On orders of the king, they were to take into captivity the two spies hiding within her home.

From that perspective, Rahab would not have had the opportunity to answer her door, hear the king's message, and then go and hide these spies.

Seriously! Think about it. The soldiers come pounding at her door. She opens the door, listens to what they have to say, and then what? Can you honestly see Rahab holding up her hand as she tells the soldiers to "hold that thought" while closing the door in their face?

With this scenario playing out in your mind, do you honestly think that she would have time to grab those two spies by the hand and run up the stairs to her roof? I cannot imagine these soldiers patiently waiting outside her door while she is up on the roof, grabbing stalks of flax to hide these men. After examining her work, satisfied that no one can tell there are two men hiding underneath, she quickly runs back down the stairs, opens the front door, and breathlessly says, "You were saying?"

Realistically, there is no way that scenario would play out. Before she could even shut the door in the soldiers' faces, they would have pushed it open, shoved her aside, and captured those men, taking her with them to certain death.

Have you ever been in the middle of telling a story when, all of a sudden, you remembered an important detail that you left out? Upon that realization, you quickly interject that detail into the story. Now that detail didn't take place where you were currently at in your story. It happened long before. You just forgot to mention it, so you just add it in and continue on with your story.

Just for the sake of argument, let's fast forward to about ten years in the future. Rahab is getting her children ready for bed. As is their nightly tradition, she asks them what story they want to hear before bedtime. She already knows in her heart the story they will ask her to tell. It's the same story she has been telling them forever, the story of the spies.

Once upon a time, long, long ago, there were these two men who came to this woman's home. Unbeknownst to them, she knew exactly who they were, which meant that the king's spies would also know who they were and, more importantly, where they were. Soon, there was a knock on her door. Soldiers were telling her of the spies and commanding her to bring them out. But she had hidden them where they couldn't find them.

"Wait. Mommy, you forgot to tell us when the lady hid the spies."

"Oh. Did I forget that part?"

You see, when the two spies showed up at Rahab's door, she knew exactly who they were. She also knew how much danger they were in. Knowing in her heart that they didn't have much time, she quickly took them to her roof. Hiding them underneath the stalks of flax, she quickly made her way down the stairs, just in time to hear the pounding on her door.

> But she had brought them up to the roof and hidden them in the stalks of flax that she had spread out on the roof. (Joshua 2:6)

45

When the king's men came to her door to take the two spies into captivity, they were already well-hidden underneath the stalks of flax. Thinking fast, Rahab told the soldiers, with an urgency in her voice, to go quickly and pursue them. If they hurried, they might just overtake them.

> So, the men pursued them on the road to the fords of the Jordan. As soon as the pursuers had gone out, they shut the gate. Now before they lay down, she came up to them on the roof. (Joshua 2:7–8)

The king's men took Rahab's advice and rushed out after the spies, having the gates of the city closed behind them, thus, ensuring that no one else could get in or out of the city.

In looking at Verse 8, we have to keep in mind that Rahab had already taken the spies upstairs to the roof. She had them lay down so she could cover them with the stalks of flax. Even if the soldiers had come to look on her roof, at a casual glance, all they would see would be the stalks of flax drying out in the sun.

So here in verse 8 when it says "before they could lay down," it wasn't referring to them hiding but rather laying down for the night.

These spies didn't just happen to land at Rahab's home. Nor did they go to her because she was a well-known prostitute. They were divinely directed by God to go to her because she had exactly what they needed, and if truth be told, they had exactly what she needed.

> Now before they lay down, she came up to them on the roof, and she said to the men: "I know that ADONAI has given you the land—dread of you has fallen on us and all the inhabitants of the land are melting in fear before you. For we have heard how ADONAI dried up the water of the Sea of Reeds before you when you came out of Egypt, and what you did to the two kings of the

Amorites that were beyond the Jordan, to Sihon and Og, whom you utterly destroyed. When we heard about it, our hearts melted and no spirit remained any more in anyone because of you. For ADONAI your God, He is God, in heaven above and on earth beneath. (Joshua 2:8–11)

Rahab began to declare to them what God had already spoken through the mouth of Moses and through the mouth of Joshua. She was simply confirming what God had already declared. In this passage, we see both the promise of possession as well as the promise of protection.

The promise of possession is "I know that ADONAI has given you the land. The promise of protection: "Dread of you has fallen on us. We are melting in fear."

Why is that? Why were they melting in fear? Why had such dread come upon them? If we are not careful, we will have missed the why behind the what. You see, Rahab disclosed to them that the inhabitants of Jericho and the surrounding nations had all heard of ADONAI.

In fact, the citizens of Jericho had been fearful of the Israelites ever since they defeated the Egyptians via the Red Sea miracle. That miracle took place forty years ago. The defeat of Sihon and Og, that victory was much more recent.

The citizens of Jericho had closely followed the exploits of the God of Abraham, Isaac, and Jacob, from the miracle of the splitting of the Red Sea forty years ago to the recent conquering of Sihon and Og.

It is no wonder that they knew the spies had entered Jericho. They had been aware of Israel's God since the day he defeated Egypt. They had been living in fear for the day that the children of Israel would show up in their land.

Israel's formidable foe, these gigantic and fierce warriors, were quivering in their boots. The land that devoured its inhabitants had no spirit left in them. Fear had melted their hearts. There was no fight left in them, not because of the children of Israel but because of the God of Israel.

By her own admission, Rahab recognized there is no god like the God of Israel. He is the only true God. ADONAI—he is God, in heaven above and on earth beneath. She then pleaded for the lives of her family to be saved.

> So now, please swear to me by ADONAI, since I have dealt kindly with you, that you will also deal kindly with my father's house. Give me a true sign that you will spare the lives of my father, my mother, my brothers, my sisters and all who belong to them, and save our lives from death. (Joshua 2:12–13)

I want you to imagine with me, for just a moment, the emotions that must have been going through Rahab the moment these two spies stepped foot into her home.

She had been following the exploits of the God of Israel. She heard the stories. Shoot, she probably had seen the pillar of cloud that overshadowed them during the day and the pillar of fire that overshadowed their camp at night.

Imagine just for a moment, Rahab going up to her roof and looking east of the Jordan, imagining a God like that caring for her, protecting her, providing for her.

You know, interestingly enough, we never find out the name of Jericho's king or the names of his men. We don't even know the names of the two spies that Joshua sent out. What we do know is the name of the prostitute who risked her life for those men. Her name was Rahab, and out of everyone in that city, God chose her.

In the gospel of John, Yeshua speaks of being chosen by God and being drawn toward God.

> You did not choose Me, but I chose you. I selected you so that you would go and produce fruit, and your fruit would remain. Then the Father will give you whatever you ask in My name. (John 15:16)

No one can come to Me unless My Father who
sent Me draws him—and I will raise him up on
the last day. (John 6:44)

Rahab was chosen by God, hand selected to carry out his mission for Jericho and the children of Israel. In the midst of her circumstances, God was drawing her to himself, which brings us to the
second Life Lesson that we can learn through the story of Joshua: *you
are not defined by your past nor your present circumstances.*

Your identity, your worth is wrapped up in the very essence of
who God is and how he sees you.

God chose Rahab and drew her to himself. In response, Rahab
truly surrendered to God. Not only was she God's choice of deliverance for the children of Israel, but as we see in the gospel of Matthew,
she was also God's choice in the lineage of Yeshua. Rahab was David's
great grandmother.[8] It was through her lineage that Messiah Yeshua
was born.

God sent those two spies to Rahab, a woman who was per-
ceptive, intelligent, and well-informed, a woman who not only con-
firmed God's promise to them but reminded them of it as well, a
woman who wasn't afraid to risk her life or her family's life in order to
protect two men she'd never met simply because theirs was the God
of heaven above and on earth beneath.

However, God also sent those men to Rahab because they had
what she needed—the only means of salvation.

The men said to her, "Our life for yours, if you
don't report this business of ours. Then it will be
when ADONAI gives us the land that we will deal
kindly and loyally with you." So, she lowered
them down by a rope through the window—for
her house was in the wall; she was living in the
wall. (Joshua 2:14–15)

Then the men said to her: "We will be released
from this oath that you have made us swear, unless

> when we come into the land, you tie this line of
> scarlet thread in the window through which you
> lowered us down, and gather to yourself in the
> house your father, your mother, your brothers
> and all your father's household. (Joshua 2:17–18)

> So, she said: "According to your words, so be it."
> Then she sent them away. After they had gone,
> she tied the scarlet cord to the window. (Joshua
> 2:21)

Who would think that a line of scarlet thread would save an entire household? Yet, Rahab wasted no time. As soon as they had gone, she tied that scarlet cord to the window. She didn't even wait until the next morning. She immediately acted upon her faith, demonstrating a simple trust and absolute confidence in God.

Rahab didn't allow her circumstances, past or present, to define her. Nor did she allow her situation to control her actions. Instead of looking to her circumstances, she looked to the God of Israel. Rahab put her trust and confidence in the God who saves. It is for this reason that Rahab became God's unexpected answer to Israel's unexpected dilemma.

Moving Forward

It had been three days since the spies were given their mission. They had now safely returned to the east side of the Jordan. Pulling Joshua aside, they began to report back to him everything that had happened, explaining to him how their cover was blown almost immediately upon entering the city. You can just imagine Joshua's shock upon hearing that the inhabitants of the land had been keeping tabs on them these forty years. They had been aware of their movements since they left Egypt. How else could you explain how they knew who the spies were and where they were staying?

As their story began to unfold, they described the bravery of this woman, a prostitute no less, who risked her life to save theirs. They would have shared how Rahab knew who they were the moment they stepped foot into her home. Yet she hid them anyway, protecting them from the king's men.

I can just picture these two men excitedly talking over one another as they finally get to the part where Rahab told them that everyone is afraid of them. Adonai has given them the land.

> "Surely Adonai has given all the land into our hands," they said to Joshua. "Indeed, all the inhabitants of the land have melted in fear before us." (Joshua 2:24)

Upon hearing those words, Joshua must have experienced a myriad of emotions—*relief, shock, awe, excitement, faith, anticipation, determination.*

- Relief in the fact that his men came back with a report of faith and not fear
- Shock over the bravery of this woman, risking her life for them
- Awed with the greatness of their God—he was doing exactly what he said he was going to do.
- Excitement over what was to come
- Faith as he hears the words "ADONAI has given us all the land"
- Anticipation over what's next and determination to do all that God says to do

At this point in their conversation, I can just see Joshua high fiving God. The God of Abraham, Isaac, and Jacob was setting things in motion to defeat their enemy and rid the land of its inhabitants. I imagine these words of God were probably resonating within his entire being.

> Every place on which the sole of your foot treads, I am giving to you, as I spoke to Moses. From the wilderness and this Lebanon to the great river, the Euphrates River—all the land of the Hittites—to the Great Sea toward the setting of the sun will be your territory. No one will be able to stand before you all the days of your life. Just as I was with Moses, so I will be with you. I will not fail you or forsake you. (Joshua 1:3–5)

With these words resonating in his heart, Joshua must have stood a bit taller, with a stance full of confidence, knowing that God was doing exactly what he said he would do.

After forty years of waiting, the time had finally come. Change was happening. They were about to transition to a new life, a new beginning.

Now, up until recently, the children of Israel had been taking their orders from Moses. But things had changed. Joshua was now their leader, and his instructions were what they need to heed.

As you know, with any change, there is a period of adjustment. That period of adjustment is a transitioning that actually ushers in additional changes, one right after another. We see that here in the opening passage of Joshua, chapter 3.

> Then Joshua rose up early in the morning, and he and all Bnei-Yisrael set out from Shittim and came to the Jordan. They lodged there before crossing over. Now it came about after three days that the officials went through the camp and they charged the people saying, "When you see the ark of the covenant of ADONAI your God and the Levitical kohanim [*priests*] carrying it, then you must set out from your place and follow it. Yet keep a distance between you and it about 2,000 cubits by measure. Don't come near it, so you may know the way by which you should go, for you haven't traveled this way before. (Joshua 3:1–4)

The first shift of change that I want to draw your attention to is where Joshua instructed them to focus their attention.

During and after the Exodus, the children of Israel were led by a pillar of cloud by day and with a pillar of fire by night to illuminate for them the way they were to go.

> ADONAI went before them in a pillar of cloud by day to lead the way and in a pillar of fire by night to give them light. So, they could travel both day and night. The pillar of cloud by day and the pil-

lar of fire by night never departed from the people. (Exodus 13:21–22)

We then see God changing things up a bit. Not only were they
being led by a pillar of cloud, but now, the ark of the covenant was
going before them, leading the way.

> So, they advanced from the mountain of ADONAI,
> a trip of three days, the Ark of the covenant of
> ADONAI going ahead of them for those three
> days to seek out a resting place for them. The
> cloud of ADONAI was over them by day when
> they advanced from the camp. Whenever the Ark
> would set out, Moses would say, "Arise, ADONAI!
> May your enemies be scattered! May those
> who hate you flee from before You!" (Numbers
> 10:33–35)

Once again, God changed things. Notice here in Joshua that
there is no mention whatsoever of the pillar of cloud going before
them. Their entire focus was to be on the ark of the covenant. Joshua
told them to watch it. When they saw the ark of the covenant and the
priests carrying it, it was then that they were to set out and follow it.
From this point on, the pillar of cloud and the pillar of fire were no
longer their covering—God was. But the truth of the matter is, God
was always their covering. The pillar of cloud and the pillar of fire
were just a physical representation of God's covering.

Things were changing. They were to no longer look to the
cloud or look to the fire for their assurance. God was with them. He
wasn't at a distance or beyond their reach. He was right there—in
their midst!

You see, the ark of the covenant was a representation of God's
royal presence and his sovereign leadership. God was their covering,
and all focus was to be on him and him alone.

He would go before them. He would lead the way. But they
would need to watch and pay close attention to where the ark was

going, for God was leading them in a direction that they had never gone before. God flat out told them:

- You haven't traveled this way before.
- This is all new to you.
- So pay attention.
- Listen closely.
- Do exactly as I tell you.

This brings us to the next Life Lesson that we can glean from Joshua, and that is this: *experiences are meant for remembering, not repeating.*

It's important that we keep in mind that the children of Israel had either experienced the splitting of the Red Sea as very small children or had heard of the splitting of the Red Sea from their parents. Either way, they knew the story well. They stood, and God acted. The sea parted, and they walked across on dry ground.

Now forty years later, they were looking at a similar body of water. No worries; they knew exactly what to expect. But that's not quite how things unfolded.

> You are to command the kohanim [*priests*] who are carrying the ark of the covenant saying: "When you reach the edge of the waters of the Jordan, you are to stand still in the Jordan." (Joshua 3:8)

> It will come to pass when the soles of the feet of the kohanim [*priests*] who are carrying the ark of ADONAI, Sovereign of all the earth, rest in the waters of the Jordan, the Jordan's waters will be cut off. The waters coming downstream will stand up in one heap. (Joshua 3:13)

Unlike the crossing of the Red Sea, the Israelites weren't instructed to simply stand and see the salvation of God. They weren't told to "Wait for it," but rather, this time around, God told Joshua to tell the *kohanim* to stand still *in* the Jordan. I can just imagine snippets of conversations spreading throughout that crowd…

"Wait a minute!"

"What?"

"No, that's not right."

"You've got it all wrong, Joshua"

"Moses didn't have us do it that way."

"Yeah, Moses said to 'Stand and see the salvation of the Lord'"

"That's right. We stood, and then the waters parted."

"He's right. The waters stood up on either side."

"Yeah, the ground was totally dry when we stepped in."

"That's right, the ground was dry, and then we crossed over."

"That's how we need to do it!"

I can just picture Joshua standing there, taking a deep breath, closing his eyes as he slightly shakes his head. The voice of God reverberating in his heart, "Chazak! Be Strong!"

In my mind's eye, I see Joshua as he stands there stroking his beard, perhaps even nodding some as he replies,

"Ah huh, that's right."

"That's exactly what God did—THEN."

"But that's not how we are doing it Now."

Experiences are meant for remembering, not repeating. They are reminders of God's goodness, God's provision, and God's faithfulness. Past experiences were never meant to replace the experiences to come. If we are not careful, we can become so focused on the method God used that we totally miss the message God is now bringing. This leads us to our next Life Lesson to be gleaned from Joshua: *our attention isn't to be focused on the* method, *but rather the Master.*

Yes, at the Red Sea crossing, they did wait until the sea split, and then they crossed over on dry ground. But not here. Here, God told the kohanim, the priests, to get their feet wet, and *then* the waters would be cut off.

Another interesting point to bring to your attention was the timing of their crossing the Jordan. It was during the *harvest* season.

At this particular time of the year, the Jordan River would have been overflowing its banks.

For those of you who have never traveled to Israel, the Jordan River is a structural depression that has the lowest elevation of any river in the world. It is more than 223 miles in length and about fifty to two hundred feet in depth. It was a raging, overflowing river. During this time in the season, it would not have been calm or peaceful. It would have been at flood levels, overflowing its bank.

The difference at the Red Sea crossing was that at that point in their lives, they didn't know the character of God. They didn't know *how* to trust him. Here, forty years later, they would have had a better understanding of God's character. Therefore, God was expecting them to trust him. In essence, God wanted them to not look back on the method used at the Red Sea but on the Master who chose that method. He is trustworthy. He is faithful.

God was telling them to step into that raging water and to simply trust him. Nothing would change until they took that step of faith. Once they stepped in, the waters stopped flowing and piled in a heap about twenty miles north near the village of Adam. The waters were also cut off at the south, near the Salt Sea.

The priests would have then proceeded to walk down into the Jordan, stopping in the middle—at its deepest depth of two hundred feet. They, along with all the children of Israel, would have had to walk down into the Jordan and up out of it.

I want to bring your attention to the Hebrew word for Jordan which is *yar-dane*, and it means "to descend into."[9] Descending into the Jordan and rising up out of the Jordan is comparable to the act of immersion or baptism—going down into and coming up out of.

Now oftentimes, when we hear of the Jordan River, we associate it with John the Immerser or John the Baptist. In the gospels of Matthew, Mark, and Luke, we read of John immersing in the Jordan River while proclaiming a message of repentance.

> In those days, John the Immerser came proclaiming in the wilderness of Judea, "Turn away from

your sins, for the kingdom of heaven is near!"
(Matthew 3:1–2)

All the Judean countryside was going out to him,
and all the Jerusalemites. As they confessed their
sins, they were being immersed by him in the
Jordan River. (Mark 1:5)

And he came into all the surrounding region of
the Jordan, proclaiming an immersion of repentance for the removal of sins. (Luke 3:3)

You were buried along with Him in immersion,
through which you also were raised with Him by
trusting in the working of God, who raised Him
from the dead. (Colossians 2:12)

Baptism or immersion is an outward representation of what has
taken place on the inside. Going down into the water represents a
dying to self, and coming up out of the water represents newness of
life.

The Israelites crossing over the Jordan, descending to its very
depths, and then rising to its highest heights was a transitional
moment in their lives. They were, in essence, leaving the old way of
life behind them and embracing newness of life.

God further instructed Joshua to choose twelve men, one from
each tribe, to take a large stone from the middle of the Jordan and
carry it across to the other side.

Take for yourself twelve men from the people,
one man from each tribe, and command them
saying, "Take for yourselves twelve stones from
the middle of the Jordan, from the place where
the feet of the kohanim [*priests*] are standing
firm, and carry them over with you, and deposit
them at the place where you will lodge tonight."

Then Joshua called the twelve men whom he had
appointed from Bnei-Yisrael, one man from each
tribe. Joshua said to them, "Cross over before the
ark of ADONAI your God into the middle of the
Jordan. Each of you, lift up a stone on his shoulder, for the number of the tribes of Bnei-Yisrael."
(Joshua 4:1–5)

When we think of the word *stone*, we more than likely picture the stones lying in our driveways or as part of the landscap-
ing. However, the stones that Joshua was speaking of were not little
stones. They were boulder-like in size and had to be carried upon
their shoulders. They would have been bulky, and they would have
been extremely heavy in weight.

I want us to pause here and take a selah moment. Stop and just
imagine with me for a moment the scene unfolding before us.

These men had to descend into the depths of the Jordan,
approximately two hundred feet. They then had to pick up boulder-like stones, lifting them up onto their shoulders where they then
had to carry them up a two-hundred-foot incline. Once they came
up out of the Jordan, they would then need to continue carrying
these boulders until they reached their destination. This was no small
task. The burdens they carried were heavy and cumbersome. The
pace that they started out with more than likely slowed with each
step that they took.

The next time you go on a walk, take a five-pound bag of pota-
toes with you. I guarantee you, by the time you reach your destination, you will have sworn that five-pound bag morphed into a
fifty-pound bag. Keep in mind that you are having to carry that bag
on your shoulders uphill the majority of the way.

With each step that they took, the weight of what they were carrying was bearing down upon them. Now imagine their relief when
they finally did reach their destination. The ark of the covenant had
found its resting place. At last, they could let go of their burdens.
What a relief they must have felt as that weight was lifted off their
shoulders.

The purpose of those stones was to be a constant reminder of what God had brought them through as well as a reminder of what he was bringing them to.

However, that wasn't the only reminder God was giving to them. Joshua was also instructed to take twelve boulder-like stones from the middle of the Jordan and to set up a memorial in that very spot where the kohanim were standing.

Again, you have to take a selah moment and think about that. Twelve boulders, large enough in size that when the waters of the Jordan returned, they would still be visible. Think about it. That would mean that they would have to extend past the two-hundred-foot depth of the Jordan River.

That would also mean that Joshua would have had to start climbing on top of those boulders in order to put yet another boulder on top of the last one he placed. Again, no easy feat. Yet it was to serve God's purpose, for this would be a constant reminder that even at their lowest point, God was with them.

At any time, they could look back and be reminded of the mighty hand of God. This would be a memorial to his goodness, his provision, and his protection as well as a constant reminder of where they came from and to where God brought them.

Letting Go

Selah moments—those moments in time where you pause, take a step back and relook at what you have just encountered. Stop. Look. Listen.

For just a moment, I want us to do exactly that. I want us to stop, listen, and look at the journey we have taken with Joshua thus far.

We have learned that with every change comes both a promise and a word of instruction. This is no ordinary promise either. It is a promise that is threefold—a promise of possession, protection, and presence.

Within the promise of possession, we've learned that God is taking you *from* something in order to bring you *to* something. In this process, this journey of change, we have the promise of protection—he is our covering. We have also received the promise of his presence—the I Am that I Am is always with us.

Even in those times when you have felt so isolated and alone, God was with you. You were never alone.

Now oftentimes, you will find that God gives you the promise long before the change occurs. When that change comes, when that time of transitioning is upon you, God reminds you of the promise he gave to you for such a time as this.

In conjunction with that threefold promise comes a set of instructions. These instructions are both foundational and situational. It is foundational in the sense that they remain the same regardless of the situation. They are instructions to:

- Be strong,
- Remember who your God is,

- Draw your strength from him continually,
- Stay connected,
- Never depart.

Those are some of the foundational instructions God has given to us. However, there are also situational instructions, instructions that are given for the current situation, for present-day circumstances. An example of a situational set of instructions would be the Red Sea crossing versus the Jordan River crossing.

The set of instructions given at the Red Sea were to stand and see the salvation of the Lord, a word of direction given as it pertained to that situation and those circumstances. However, at the Jordan River, the word of direction that was given at that time was to step out into the water, and then they would see what God would do. In both situations, there was change, promise, and instruction.

As our journey took us to Jericho, we learned that you and I are not defined by our past or present circumstances. Your identity, your worth is wrapped up in the very essence of *who* God is. You are who he says you are. The only thing that matters is what God thinks of you. Just because things have always been this way doesn't mean they will stay this way.

God is in control of your circumstances, and when you truly surrender to what he is wanting to form in you, you will begin to see his goodness unfold in the midst of even the most adverse of circumstances.

Another life-changing lesson that we've learned as we've traveled with Joshua is that our experiences were meant for remembering, not repeating. Your past experiences are simply reminders of God's goodness, provision, and faithfulness. Your past was never meant to replace your present or future experiences with God.

On the heels of those truths, we have learned that our attention isn't to be focused on the method but, rather, upon the Master. Methods will change. However, the God of those methods will not. If we are not careful, we could become so focused on the method God used yesterday that we totally miss the message God is bringing today.

Selah moments oftentimes become defining moments in our lives. Now that we've paused, listened, and taken in what God has shown us, let us continue in our journey.

Joshua and the children of Israel had finally arrived. After all these years, they were now standing upon the very ground ADONAI their God had promised them. Yet it wasn't at the western banks of the Jordan where their burdens were released. Bnei-Yisrael traveled on until they reached Gilgal. It was there that they would set up camp. It was there where they would set up their memorial to God.

> Now the people came up from the Jordan on the tenth day of the first month and camped at Gilgal on the eastern border of Jericho. Those twelve stones, which they had taken out of the Jordan, Joshua set up in Gilgal. (Joshua 4:19–20)

I want to bring your attention to the Hebrew word *Gilgal,* which means "a rolling away. "[10] The meaning of this word is significant on many levels. Not only is it a reminder of the rolling away of the waters of the Jordan, but it also signifies a rolling away of the burdens they carried, burdens that went beyond the boulders which were carried upon the shoulders of those twelve men.

Keep in mind that in order to cross over, they would need to descend into the Jordan and rise up out of it in order to reach the other side. Once again, this act was comparable to the act of immersion or baptism. It was a representation of both dying to self and being raised to newness of life.

This crossing over into newness of life also entailed a relinquishing of the burdens that were carried before and during that transition. In other words, all the burdens, shame, and reproach that were associated with their previous life were to be let go of. Everything associated with their former lifestyle, God was relieving them of those burdens.

God was both figuratively and literally relieving their shoulder from the burden they carried. Just as those men had to let go of and lay down those boulders, so we, too, must let go of and lay down our burdens.

> Commit your way to ADONAI, Trust in Him, and
> He will do it. (Psalm 37:5)

Surprisingly enough, this word *commit* doesn't mean to be loyal or to be faithful. In fact, it doesn't even mean to be committed.

The original Hebrew word used in this text is the word *galal*, and it means "to roll away." This word is referring to pushing our will and our way of doing things out of the way.

The only way we can do that is by trusting him in the process, trusting that he will do it.

He will give us the strength that we need. He will give us the courage to let go of the past, to relinquish our mindset of doing things our way.

That boulder, those burdens which you have been carrying, are made up of all the particles of your past hurts, disappointments, shortcomings, and failures. It's time to lay them down. When you do, you will find that when you look back, you will see a memorial reminding you of what God has delivered you from.

He will relieve our shoulders from the burden as we roll away our ways of doing things to cling to his will, his way always, which brings us to the fifth Life Lesson that we can take away from our journey with Joshua: *it has to be his will, his way, always.*

This Life Lesson goes hand in hand with the previous lesson we learned. Our focus is to be on the Master, not on his methods. It has to be his will, his way, always. No exceptions.

The next nugget of truth that I want to draw your attention to is the timing of their arrival.

> Now the people came up from the Jordan on the
> tenth day of the first month and camped at Gilgal
> on the eastern border of Jericho. (Joshua 4:19)

God is very detail oriented. He specifically tells us when they stepped onto the Promised Land. They arrived on the other side of the Jordan on the tenth day of the first month. We know from Scripture that it was during the harvest season.

The first month, being the month of Nisan,[11] would make this the *barley harvest* which would mean that the crossing of the Jordan took place during the Feast Season of *Pesach*.

> Now ADONAI spoke to Moses and Aaron in the land of Egypt saying, "This month will mark the beginning of months for you; it is to be the first month of the year for you. Tell all the congregation of Israel that on the tenth day of this month, each man is to take a lamb for his family one lamb for the household." (Exodus 12:1–4)

The next point of interest in our journey is the response of the nations to their arrival.

> Now it came about when all the Amorite kings beyond the Jordan westward and all the Canaanite kings by the sea heard how ADONAI had dried up the waters of the Jordan before Bnei-Yisrael until they had crossed, their heart melted, nor was there any spirit in them anymore, because of Bnei-Yisrael. (Joshua 5:1)

This would have been the perfect time for them to go out and defeat their enemies. All of the kings, both of the Amorites and the Canaanites, had heard about ADONAI and not just what he had done forty years ago at the Red Sea or what they had done several months back to Sihon and Og, whom they utterly destroyed.

These kings knew what ADONAI had *just* accomplished at the Jordan River. Remember, they had spies of their own, keeping tabs on the children of Israel. Even in that day and age, word spread fast. It would be safe to surmise that even before the Israelites finished setting up camp at Gilgal, word would have reached these kings of how the God of Israel had cut off the raging waters of the Jordan.

This wasn't a miracle of days gone by. That just happened, alerting them to the truth that the God of Israel was still with them, fighting their battles and doing the impossible. They were paralyzed with fear, making this a great and strategic time for Israel to go in and defeat their enemy when this miracle was still fresh in their minds.

But God had something else in mind. Instead of instructions to prepare for war, Joshua was given instructions to circumcise all the men of Israel.

> At that time ADONAI said to Joshua, "Make yourself flint knives and circumcise again Bnei-Yisrael a second time." So, Joshua made flint knives and circumcised Bnei-Yisrael at Gibeath-ha-araloth. (Joshua 5:2–3)

This is one of those selah moments, a time to stop and think about the timing of this word of instruction.

Their arrival to the west of the Jordan, east of Jericho, was during the Feast Season of Pesach, a Feast Season that incorporates three individual feasts: Passover or Pesach, the Feast of Matzah or Unleavened Bread, and First Fruits.

> These are the appointed feasts of ADONAI, holy convocations which you are to proclaim in their appointed season. During the first month, on the fourteenth day of the month in the evening, is ADONAI's Passover. (Leviticus 23:4–5)

> When you come into the land which ADONAI will give you as He has promised, you are to keep this ceremony. (Exodus 12:25)

In the seventeenth chapter of Genesis, we read where God made his covenant pledge to Abraham. The sign of that covenant was circumcision.[12] Scripture also tells us that only those who were circumcised could participate in the Feast of Passover.

> But if an outsider dwells with you, who could keep the Passover for ADONAI, all his males must be circumcised. Then let him draw near and keep it. He will be like one who is native to the land. But no uncircumcised person may eat from it. (Exodus 12:48)

The circumcision here in Joshua was a renewing of the *covenant*. A modern-day example of this would be of a husband and wife who had been married for forty years renewing their vows, once again exchanging rings as a sign of that marriage covenant. This couple wouldn't be making a new covenant but, rather, renewing the previous covenant that they had already made.

> Now this is the reason why Joshua circumcised: all the people that came out of Egypt who were males—all the men of war—had died after they came out of Egypt. Though all the people that came out were circumcised, none of the people who were born in the wilderness along the way as they came out of Egypt had been circumcised. For Bnei-Yisrael walked 40 years in the wilderness, until all the—nation's men of war who came out of Egypt died out, because they had not listened to the voice of ADONAI. To them ADONAI had sworn that He would never let them see the land which ADONAI had sworn to their fathers that He would give us, a land flowing with milk and honey. But He raised up their children in their place. Joshua circumcised them, for they were uncircumcised, since they had not been circumcised along the way. (Joshua 5:4–7)

God was renewing his covenant promise that he made to Abraham that extended all the way to the descendants who had just crossed over the Jordan. Circumcision had to take place in preparation for honoring the command of keeping the Passover once they had entered the Promised Land.

Talk about complete vulnerability. Every male from newborn to the aged were circumcised which meant that every man of war was incapacitated. They were completely vulnerable.

Think about this, look at how quickly word spread about the two spies entering Jericho or how quickly word got out concerning the cutting back of the waters of the Jordan. With that in mind, it wouldn't be any stretch of the imagination to say that word spread just as quickly regarding the army of Israel being totally incapacitated. I can just imagine the conversations flowing around the dinner table that night...

"I'm sorry, what did you say?"

"They did what?" (Every man hearing this news instinctively crosses his legs in pure protective reflex.)

"You're not serious?"

"You're kidding me, right?"

This would have been the perfect time to defeat the army of Israel when there would be nothing that they could do to stop them. Yet not one of these armies rose up against Israel.

Bnei-Yisrael knew they were vulnerable. The enemy armies knew they were vulnerable. Yet this wasn't about the armies of the land—this was about Israel recognizing who was truly responsible for their many victories.

God was their protector. He was their vindicator. It was ADONAI who split the Red Sea, not Moses.

It was ADONAI who cut off the waters, not Joshua. It was *ADONAI Elohim* and him alone.

Their trust had to be in God. The temptation to think they were "all that" upon hearing the response of their arrival would have been great.

Every enemy warrior was stricken with fear. The men of Israel could have wiped them out. However, if that had happened, their rejoicing could have easily centered around their own accomplishments and fighting skills. The temptation to take credit for striking fear in the hearts of their enemies would have been great.

Pride and arrogance could have quickly replaced a heart of humility and meekness. This brings us to the next Life Lesson that we can learn from our journey with Joshua: *it was ADONAI, it has always been ADONAI, and it will always be ADONAI—his strength, his protection, his provision, his intervention, his power, his authority, his doing.*

The very act of crossing over the Jordan represented a dying to self. Descending into the depths of the Jordan and coming up out of the Jordan was leaving the old and embracing the new.

They had left Egypt, but now Egypt had to leave them. There needed to be a letting go and a cutting away of the flesh so that they could truly go and accomplish all that God had for them to accomplish.

Even though their parents and grandparents had left Egypt, Egypt had never truly left them. They were constantly reverting back to life in Egypt, pining away for the "good ole' days," the *what ifs* and *if onlys* chipping away at the little faith that had been gradually building up within them.

This circumcision was not only a covenant renewal, but it served as a reminder that Egypt was never their home, regardless of the fact that generation after generation after generation lived there. It was never their home.

It was on the other side of the Jordan where they found a newness of life that provided both renewal and removal.

> Then ADONAI said to Joshua, "This day I have rolled away the reproach of Egypt from you." Therefore, the name of that place has been called Gilgal to this day. (Joshua 5:9)

Reproach—this word is derived from the Hebrew word *cherpah*, which means "the condition of shame and disgrace."[13]

Looking at the spiritual significance of circumcision, a cutting away of the flesh brings with it a removal of the shame and disgrace your flesh puts on you.

Egypt represents our life apart from God—it represents our flesh. When we are removed from Egypt, and Egypt is removed from us, there is a renewing that takes place.

Again, the old is passed away, and behold, the fresh and the new has come. All the shame and all the disgrace that followed the Israelites from Egypt was rolled away at that moment.

They could look back at the center of the Jordan River and see that at their lowest point, God was in their midst.

They could look at the memorial on the other side of the Jordan in Gilgal and have a reminder of what God had brought them through and what he was bringing them to.

Truth be told, they would also have a constant reminder in their flesh of the covenant that God had renewed with them—that he was and is faithful to keep his promises.

> Now it came to pass after they had finished circumcising the entire nation, they remained in their places in the camp until they recovered. Then ADONAI said to Joshua, "This day I have rolled away the reproach of Egypt from you." Therefore, the name of that place has been called Gilgal to this day. While Bnei-Yisrael camped at Gilgal, they observed Passover on the evening of the fourteenth day of the month in the plains of Jericho. On the day after the Passover, on that very day, they ate of the produce of the land, matzot [*unleavened bread*] and roasted grain. Then the manna ceased on the day after they had eaten of the produce of the land. Bnei-Yisrael had manna no longer, but ate some of the yield of the land of Canaan that year. (Joshua 5:8–12)

Everything associated with their wilderness experience had now ceased, including the gathering of manna, for it was in the midst of their healing—both physically and spiritually—that they celebrated the Passover meal and rejoiced over the partaking of the firstfruits of the land.

Letting go, rolling away—actions that usher in a newness of life along with an awakening of the new beginnings that lie just ahead.

Choosing Sides

All was quiet in Gilgal. The celebration of Passover, a reminder of God's salvation and deliverance, had been completed. With the men of Israel still recovering from their circumcision, our journey takes us outside the camp at Gilgal. Joshua, God's appointed commander of Israel, had gone for a long walk.

Knowing that Joshua was a man of prayer, it wouldn't be a stretch of the imagination to think of this as a prayer walk. As commander and leader of God's people, it would make sense that Joshua would be seeking God's direction on how to go about breaching the impregnable walls of Jericho. From the time that the spies' entrance into Jericho was discovered, the city had been tightly shut up—no one was going out, and no one was coming in. Joshua needed a game plan.

They didn't have at their disposal battering rams, catapults, scaling ladders, or even moving towers. What they did have at their disposal was an array of swords, arrows, slings, and spears, none of which could penetrate Jericho's walls. His experience fighting the Amalekites was all well and good, once he was behind the walls. Therein lies the dilemma. How do they get behind those walls? That is the backdrop of our opening scene.

> Now it came to pass when Joshua was near Jericho that he lifted up his eyes and looked, and behold, there was a man standing in front of him with his sword drawn in his hand. Joshua approached him and said to him: "Are you for us or for our adversaries?" (Joshua 5:13)

Joshua was standing near Jericho, and he was alone. Everyone else was at camp. Scripture alludes to the fact that he was looking down, again whether in contemplation, prayer, or a mixture of both, when something catches his attention. Looking up, he saw a man standing there in front of him with his sword drawn. Joshua recognized this as the military stance that it was.

You see, standing with any weapon drawn is a military position of one who is either standing guard or who is standing ready to go against a foe defensively or offensively. Standing with his sword drawn would suggest to Joshua that this man was there to fight either against Israel, with Israel, or for Israel.

What's so interesting here is Joshua's initial response to such an encounter. He didn't run. He didn't retreat. He didn't even draw his own weapon, nor did he shrink back in fear. Joshua didn't do any of those things. Instead, he actually approached this man.

For just a moment, I want us to pause here and take a selah moment. When Joshua first took on the leadership of God's people, God repeatedly told Joshua, "Chazak! Be strong, be courageous."

This word *courageous* comes from the Hebrew word *amats* which means to be "brave and bold, determined and alert."[14]

After several times of God repeating these words to Joshua, he told him not to be afraid and gave him this promise.

> Have I not commanded you? Chazak! Be strong!
> Do not be terrified or dismayed, for ADONAI your
> God is with you wherever you go. (Joshua 1:9)

Within that short time span of a few weeks, there was an inner transformation that took place in Joshua. On the eastern banks of the Jordan, Joshua felt fear and anxiety over what God was calling him to do.

Since that time, Joshua had seen the waters of the Jordan stand in one heap on either side of him. He had crossed over the Jordan River on dry ground and had experienced firsthand the protective covering of God as all the men of war had been incapacitated through circumcision.

He had also experienced the faithfulness of God as he partook of the firstfruits of the land during the Passover celebration.

Joshua had grown in his experiential knowledge of *who* God is and *what* God can accomplish. He was no longer afraid as he knew without a doubt that God is true to his word. If he said it, he will do it. If he promised, it will surely come to pass.

God promised Joshua that he would never be alone, for God would be with him everywhere he went.

To the naked eye, it would have appeared that Joshua was alone that night when he encountered this warrior. But Joshua knew better. He was never alone—God was right there, which brings us to the next Life Lesson that we can glean from Joshua: *even when our own eyes can't see, God is there; he is always right there.*

This was the very promise that Joshua received prior to taking over the leadership of God's people.

> Chazak! Be courageous! Do not be afraid or tremble before them. For ADONAI your God—He is the One who goes with you. He will not fail you or abandon you. Then Moses summoned Joshua and said to him in the sight of all Israel, "Be strong! Be courageous! For you are to go with this people into the land ADONAI has sworn to their fathers to give them, and you are to enable them to inherit it. ADONAI—He is the One who goes before you. He will be with you. He will not fail you or abandon you. Do not fear or be discouraged." (Deuteronomy 31:6–8)

God then reiterated this same promise after Joshua stepped into his leadership role, assuring him that he would be with him wherever he went.

The writer of Hebrews reminds us of this very truth in Hebrews 13:5b which reads, "I will never leave you or forsake you."

Joshua had experienced God's presence with him. There was no doubt in his heart that God was right there with him, even as he faced this mysterious warrior.

It was for that reason that he boldly approached the man with the drawn sword and flat out asked, "Are you for us? Or for our enemies?"

Joshua wanted to know whether or not this man was friend or foe—"Whose side are you on?"

At this point in this mysterious encounter, Joshua didn't know who this man truly was. However, that would change as Joshua heard this man's response.

> "Neither," he said. "Rather, I have now come as commander of ADONAI's army." Then Joshua fell on his face to the ground and worshipped. Then he asked him, "What is my lord saying to his servant?" Then the commander of ADONAI's army replied to Joshua, "Take your sandal off of your foot, for the place where you are standing is holy." And Joshua did so. (Joshua 5:14–15)

This man revealed his identity as the commander of God's army. In essence, he was telling Joshua, "I AM the God of angel armies."

There are some Bible translations that use the phrasing *Lord of hosts*. Both phrases are derived from the Hebrew name *ADONAI-Tzva'ot*. God is named according to his character.

> Thus, says ADONAI, who gives the sun as a light by day and the fixed order of the moon and the stars as a light by night, who stirs up the sea so its waves roar, ADONAI-Tzva'ot is His Name. (Jeremiah 31:34)

In Isaiah's prophesy of the coming Messiah, he calls him Mighty God, *El Gibbor* in Hebrew.[15] This speaks of a mighty warrior God.

The Hebrew word *gibbor* means "strong or mighty" and refers to someone who is bold, strong, and valiant on and off the battlefield.[16]

We see this same name in the story of David when he was facing the Philistine giant, Goliath.

> Then David said to the Philistine, "You are com-
> ing to me with a sword, a spear and a javelin, but
> I am coming to you in the Name of ADONAI-
> Tzva'ot, God of the armies of Israel, whom you
> have defied." (1 Samuel 17:45)

Joshua's response to this declaration was utterly appropriate. He immediately fell on his face and worshiped at his feet. If this were a man or an angel, they would have immediately repelled Joshua's worshipful response. We see a perfect example of this in the book of Acts.

When Paul and Barnabas were in Lystra, proclaiming the Good News of Messiah, they came upon a man who was crippled from birth. While this man was listening to the message Paul preached, his faith grew. This simple trust and absolute confidence in God's word was evident to Paul. This man believed.

> When Paul looked intently at him and saw that he
> had faith to be healed, he said with a loud voice,
> "Stand right up! On your feet!" And the man leaped
> up and began to walk around! (Acts 14:9–10)

This man was immediately healed. The crowds went wild. They believed Paul to be one of the gods that came down to them. The people of that city began to bring garlands and bulls with the intention of sacrificing them to Paul and Barnabas.

As soon as Paul and Barnabas heard that they were trying to worship them as gods, they immediately put a stop to it, declaring that they were men just like them.

> But when the emissaries [*apostles*] Barnabas
> and Paul heard of it, they tore their clothes and

rushed out among the crowd, crying out and saying, "Men, why are you doing these things? We too are human, just like you! We proclaim the Good News to you, telling you to turn from these worthless things to the living God, who made the heaven and the earth and the sea and all that is in them." (Acts 14:14–15)

Another example can be found in Revelation, chapter 19, only this time, it has to deal with an angel of the Lord.

Then I fell down at his feet and worshipped him. But he said to me, "See that you do not do that—for I am only a fellow servant with you and your brothers and sisters who hold to the testimony of Yeshua. Worship God! For the testimony of Yeshua is the Spirit of Prophesy. (Revelation 19:10)

Yet here in Joshua, we don't see his worship being stopped or prevented but, rather, welcomed and accepted. Joshua had indeed met the preincarnate Yeshua Messiah, who does indeed command the armies or hosts of heaven.

We actually get a glimpse of this vast army that he commands when Aram was at war against Israel.

The story opens with the king of Aram furious with his own officers. There was a mole within his camp. How else could you explain Israel being two steps ahead of them with each and every attempt to attack? The king was determined to draw out the mole and kill him on the spot. However, it wasn't a traitor that was exposing their strategies to the king of Israel. It was a prophet. Not just any prophet either. This man was a prophet for the God of Israel.

Enraged with this news, the king changed his plans. Forget attacking the army of Israel. His new target was a prophet named Elisha, to find him and kill him.

With orders from the king, this Aramean army traveled all night with the intent of seizing the prophet of God. Horses, chariots, and soldiers surrounded the city where Elisha, the man of God, and his servant were staying.

Imagine waking up to this scene, innocently leaving your tent in the wee hours of the morning to begin your day. It wasn't a lion or bear greeting you but, rather, the largest army you have ever seen.

> Now when the attendant of the man of God had risen early and gone out, behold, an army with horses and chariots was surrounding the city. So, his attendant said to him, "Alas, my master! What are we going to?" "Fear not," he replied, "for those who are with us are more than those who are with them." Then Elisha prayed and said, "ADONAI, please open his eyes that he may see." Then ADONAI opened the eyes of the young man and he saw, and behold, the mountain was full of horses and chariots of fire all around Elisha. (2 Kings 6:15–17)

The fiery armies of heaven surrounded their camp, guarding them and protecting them from the enemies that were coming against them. Elisha's word to his servant was, "Fear not, for those who are with us are more than those who are with them."

Even the gospel of Luke describes this formidable host as a multitude of heavenly armies. It wasn't just a great army like that of Aram. It was a multitude of fiery armies from heaven.

This glimpse into the armies of heaven is further expanded to us in the *revelation* of Yeshua where we not only see a description of the fiery armies of heaven but a small glimpse of their Commander, Yeshua Messiah.

> Then I saw heaven opened, and behold, a white horse! The One riding on it is called Faithful and True, and He judges and makes war in righ-

teousness. His eyes are like a flame of fire, and many royal crowns are on His head. He has a name written that no one knows except Himself. He is clothed in a robe dipped in blood, and the very name by which He is called is "the Word of God." And the armies of heaven, clothed in fine linen, white and clean, following Him on white horses. From His mouth comes a sharp sword— so that with it He may strike down the nations— and He shall rule them with an iron rod, and He treads the winepress of the furious wrath of *Elohei-Tzva'ot.* (Revelation 19:11–16)

He is ADONAI-Tzva'ot, the Lord of hosts, the Lord of lords, the King of kings, and he has come to deliver a word to Joshua!

The military stance of the Commander of God's army was one of authority, power, and command. He stood with sword drawn— again, a military position that speaks of one standing guard, ready to go up against the enemy.

We can't lose sight of what was going on back at the camp in Gilgal. All the men of war were still healing and recuperating from surgery. There were no men guarding the camp or protecting the women and children.

As quickly as word spread concerning the children of Israel, you know that word had gotten back to the Amorite and Canaanite kings of their present condition. Yet not a single king or enemy of the land attacked them.

I can easily imagine God opening their eyes, like he did for the servant of Elisha, giving those kings just a small glimpse at the armies of heaven that were guarding the camp of Israel.

Unlike Elisha, Joshua didn't see the armies of heaven surrounding the camp of Israel. He had, however, come face-to-face with the Commander himself. Know this, where the Commander is, the army is not far off.

I do want to pause here and revisit the question Joshua asked and the answer that he received.

Joshua 5:13b reads, "Are you for us or for our adversaries?" To which, the Commander of ADONAI's army replied "Neither."

Oftentimes when we are in a conflict, we want God to choose our side…after all, we're the ones who are right. We know backward and forward the promise in Romans 8:31 that says, "If God is for us, who can be against us?"

If we are not careful, we will use that verse, whether consciously or unconsciously, against another brother or sister whom we are not getting along with, which brings us to our next Life Lesson: *God never chooses sides as he is always on the side of* righteousness. That will never change.

You see, God doesn't want us standing across from him. He wants us standing next to him. God never changes. He always stands on the side of *righteousness*. It is up to us to choose where we stand. The question is, are we upholding his righteous cause or trying to make him uphold ours?

Oftentimes in our relationships, we are so bent on being right that we are quite willing to forfeit the relationship just to get a win. That is not the heart of God.

We must come to the place in our lives where we would rather be in right relationship than to be "right." It's not about choosing sides; it's about being righteous and maintaining his righteous cause. And Joshua got that.

> Then Joshua fell on his face to the ground and worshipped. Then he asked him, "What is my lord saying to his servant?" Then the commander of ADONAI's army replied to Joshua, "Take your sandal off of your foot, for the place where you are standing is holy." And Joshua did so. (Joshua 5:14b–15)

Joshua worshipped him and then humbly asked for wisdom and direction. God then repeated a similar set of instructions that he gave to Moses back at the burning bush.

When ADONAI saw that he turned to look, He called to him out of the midst of the bush and said, "Moses, Moses!" So, he answered, "Hineni." [*Here I am.*] Then He said, "Come no closer. Take your sandals off your feet, for the place where you are standing is holy ground." (Exodus 3:4–5)

Joshua received this same set of instructions. He was in the presence of pure holiness. God wanted no barrier between his holiness and the men he had chosen. So he instructed them to remove the very thing that had become a barrier between them. Remove your sandals. It is in this place of humility and total surrender that Joshua received the very answer he was seeking. As he left the camp at Gilgal, he was very likely praying along these lines:

"God, give me wisdom."

"Show me how you want us to attack Jericho."

"God, please reveal to me the way to conquer this city."

"Show me the way."

"Help me to understand what it is that you want me to do."

Right there, on the outskirts of Jericho, God revealed his plan to Joshua. Step by step, ADONAI laid out before Joshua his battle plan, right down to the smallest of details.

God's Battle Plan

Dread had filled the city of Jericho. No one was getting in, and no one was getting out. The city had been tightly shut up ever since the spies of Israel had infi

ltrated it. Without the use of battering rams, catapults, scaling ladders, or even moving towers, it would be humanly impossible to breach the impregnable walls of that city—the operative phrase here being *humanly impossible*. So God simply reminded Joshua of the promise he had already given to him.

> Then Adonai said to Joshua, "Look, I have given Jericho into your hand, with its king and mighty warriors." (Joshua 6:2)

Some Bible translations use the word *see* in place of the word *look*. Either way, the Hebrew word is *ra'ah*, and it means "to see, perceive and to have vision."[17]

In essence, God opened Joshua's eyes, enabling him to see the end from the beginning. The prophet Isaiah spoke of this very thing.

> Do not dread or be afraid. Have I not told you and declared it long ago? So, you are My witnesses! Is there any God beside Me? Is there any other Rock? I know of none. (Isaiah 44:8)

> Remember the former things of old; For I am God—there is no other. I am God, and there is none like Me—declaring the end from the begin-

ning, from ancient time, what is yet to come, saying, "My purpose will stand, and I will accomplish all that I please." (Isaiah 46:9–10)

It really doesn't matter what is standing in front of us when
God is standing beside us. Nor does it matter the size of the obstacle
before us, for God is greater still. This leads us to the next Life Lesson
that we can glean from Joshua, and that is this: *you are to see this* fight
from the victory *and proceed accordingly*

As we continue on here in our journey, God begins to unfold
his step-by-step plan to Joshua.

> Now you are to march around the city, all the
> men of war circling the city once. So, you are to
> do for six days. Seven kohanim [*priests*] will carry
> seven Shofarot [*trumpets*] of rams' horns before
> the ark. Then on the seventh day you are to circle
> the city seven times while the kohanim blow the
> Shofarot. It will be when they make a long blast
> with the rams' horn, when you hear the sound
> of the shofar, have all the people shout a loud
> shout—then the wall of the city will fall down
> flat, and the people will go up, everyone straight
> ahead. (Joshua 6:3–5)

God revealed his plan to Joshua who then in turn gave instruction to the children of Israel. Joshua summoned the kohanim and
gave them their set of instructions.

The armed force of Israel was to lead the way. Following them
would be seven of the kohanim carrying the *shofarot* of rams' horns
before the ark. Their job was to blow the seven shofarot continually. The next group of kohanim would be the ones carrying the ark.
They in turn would be followed by the rear guard and then the rest
of Israel.

Joshua's instruction to the children of Israel was to move forward, marching around the city in silence. No sound was to be heard except for the sounding of the shofarot.

> Then he said to the people, "Move forward, march around the city, and let the armed force march ahead of the ark of ADONAI. (Joshua 6:7)

> But Joshua ordered the people saying: "You must not shout nor let your voice be heard nor let a word proceed out of your mouth, until the Day I tell you 'shout!' Then you will shout. (Joshua 6:10)

One thing that I want to draw your attention to is that the instruction they received wasn't to simply walk around the city but rather to march around it.

According to *Webster's Dictionary* the word *march* means to "move along steadily usually with a rhythmic stride and in step with others." It also means to "move in a direct purposeful manner; to make steady progress."[18]

They weren't just taking a stroll around the city. They had a purpose, and they were in unity. With every step that they took, the promise God had spoken to them was probably resonating within each and every one of them: "Every place on which the sole of your foot treads, I am giving to you, as I spoke to Moses."[19]

Every step they took spoke of possession, protection, and presence. God was very specific in his directions. They were to march around the city of Jericho, encircling it once, for six days.

The second thing I want to draw your attention to are the numbers six and seven. They were instructed to march around the city of Jericho once every day for six days. The number six represents *man*. Scripture tells us that we are colaborers with God, partnering with him in carrying out his plans and purposes.[20] We see exactly that happening here in Joshua. The children of Israel had their part to play, and God had his.

The next number that we see is the number seven—seven kohanim, seven shofarot, the seventh day, and the seventh time. The number seven represents both perfection and completeness. These were their marching orders:

- The armed forces of Israel was to go before the seven kohanim.
- The seven kohanim were to go before the ark of ADONAI.
- The rear guard was to then come behind the ark of the covenant.
- The rest of the people were then to follow.

If we are not careful, we could easily miss the significance of the blowing of the shofarot. You see, at a causal glance, you could easily think that they marched around the city once for six days. Then on the seventh day, they marched around the city seven times. On that seventh time, the kohanim blew the shofar with a loud blast, and the walls came tumbling down.

Here's the thing; that's not how this played out. Scripture tells us that the kohanim blew the shofarot continually all seven days.

> And it was so. After Joshua had spoken to the people, seven kohanim [*priests*] carrying the seven Shofarot [*trumpets*] of rams' horns before ADONAI went forward and blew the Shofarot, and the ark of the covenant of ADONAI followed them. Also, the armed force went before the kohanim who blew the Shofarot, and the rear guard came behind the ark, while the Shofarot continued to blow. (Joshua 6:8–9)

There was a continual blowing of the shofarot. In order to help us better understand the significance of the blowing of the shofarot, we need to have a deeper understanding of the various blasts.

There are four distinct sounds associated with the blowing of the shofar. These sounds are interpreted as follows:

- The *tekiah* is one long blast.
  - This was the call to attention.
- The *teruah* are nine staccato blasts.
  - This was an alarm.
  - Get ready.
- The *shevarim* are three wave-like blasts.
  - A call to stand by the banner of God
  - Pay attention
  - Something is about to happen
- The *tekiah gedolah* is one prolonged blast that grows with intensity.
  - Signifying the King is in our midst

For six days, the Israelites would set out from camp and begin their march, encircling the city of Jericho. The order of this procession would be:

- The armed forces of Israel leading the way
- Followed by the seven kohanim blowing the shofarot
- Next comes the ark of ADONAI
- Followed by the rear guard
- Last but not least were the remaining Israelites

The blowing of the shofarot would consist of the first three soundings:

- The tekiah
  - one long blast
  - the call to attention
- Teruah
  - nine staccato blasts
  - the signal to get ready

- Shevarim (three wave-like blasts)
  o   pay attention
  o   something's about to happen

These were the blasts that continued to sound the entire time they were marching and encircling the city. This sounding of the shofar would have instilled faith in the hearts of the children of Israel. At the same time, it would have instilled fear into the hearts of those living beyond the walls.

> If a shofar alarm sounds in a city, will people not tremble? (Amos 3:6a)

With each sounding of the shofar, the enemies' resolve weakened. With heightened emotions, the mighty warriors of Jericho waited in readiness for the attack—the attack that never came.

Every day for six days, they prepared themselves for war, hearing the continual sounding of the shofar, waiting in anxiety for the God of angel armies to attack.

Poised for attack, ready to fight, they were suddenly met with silence. The troops of Israel were leaving.

Can you imagine the relief, the sense of reprieve, only to be greeted the next morning once again with the continual sounding of the shofar? Talk about psychological warfare. By day seven, they must have been a nervous wreck.

Let's take a selah moment and just think about this. Scripture tells us that while Israel was still camped west of the Jordan, the inhabitants of the land were filled with dread. They were melting in fear, and there was no spirit left in them, all because they had heard of what happened to the two kings of the Amorites, Sihon and Og.

You can only imagine the fear that had now gripped their hearts knowing that the God of Israel had them in his sight. They were now the object of God's full attention.

Day seven arrived. It started out the same as all the previous days, only the sounding of the shofarot didn't stop. It kept sounding and sounding and sounding. It didn't let up. Nor did it lessen in its intensity. Nor did the army leave after its first circle around. They were not stopping but had continued to circle and circle and circle. They were not stopping. The sounding of the shofarot was not stopping.

Up until this point, the sounding of the shofar had been the tekiah, shevarim, and the teruah. However, the children of Israel knew what was coming. They had been instructed. For six days, the people hadn't made a sound. On the seventh day, they still hadn't made a sound. No voice was heard. No whisper was made. But all of that was about to change.

The Israelites knew what was coming. On the seventh circuit, when they heard the kohanim blow the shofarot sounding the tekiah gedolah, signifying the King was in their midst, they were to shout!

> So, when the Shofarot blew, the people shouted. When the people heard the sound of the shofar [*the Tekiah Gedolah*] the people shouted a loud shout—and the wall fell down flat! So, the people went up into the city, everyone straight ahead, and they captured the city. (Joshua 6:20)

This wasn't a one-two-three kind of event. This happened simultaneously. The tekiah gedolah sounded. The people shouted. The walls came down.

For just a moment, I want to bring your attention to the walls. I don't know about you, but I had always thought that when the people shouted, the walls just crumbled. But that's not what happened.

Scripture tells us that the wall fell down flat. This city was surrounded by a wall, and God just pushed that sucker down as easily as if it was a domino. The children of Israel simply ran over the walls. They didn't have to mess with trying to run through the wreckage of broken rocks and crumbling boulders. God knocked them down flat. The only walls that remained standing and untouched were the four walls of Rahab's house.

> Then Joshua said to the two men who had spied out the land: "Go into the harlot's house and

bring the woman and all who belong to her, as you swore to her." So, the young spies went in and brought out Rahab, her father, her mother, her relatives and all who belonged to her. All her relatives they brought out and put them outside the camp of Israel. (Joshua 6:22–23)

Rahab was given a promise back when the children of Israel were still on the western banks of the Jordan. She had interceded for her family, boldly asking for the lives of her:

- Father and mother,
- Her brothers and sisters,
- And all who belonged to them,
- Sister-in-laws,
- Brother-in-laws,
- Children,
- And perhaps even their parents and siblings.

God heard her request and promised to save her and her entire household, a promise that has been extended to you and I.

Put your trust in the Lord Yeshua and you will be saved—you and your household. (Acts 16:31)

That was exactly what God did for Rahab, which brings us to the next Life Lesson in this journey with Joshua, and that is this: *earnestly wait for his plans to develop regarding you.*

Rahab had no idea how long it was going to be before the God of Israel came to her rescue. What she did know was once she sent the spies away, she had three days to convince her family to move in with her.

They had to be with her, in her home, in order to be saved. It probably seemed like forever since the time the spies left until they crossed over the Jordan.

What she thought would only be a few short days turned out to be a lot longer. I mean, just stop and think about it. I can just imagine Rahab going up to her rooftop and overlooking the Jordan, waiting in anticipation for the Israelites to cross over. I can imagine the excitement she must have felt either upon hearing or even possibly seeing the waters of the Jordan standing to one side, witnessing the camp of Israel crossing over on dry ground, knowing that any day, they were coming to her rescue.

Yet nothing happened. Then she heard news about the men being circumcised and then hearing the sounds of celebration as they partook of Passover.

Rahab would have had plenty of time to doubt and question whether or not God had forgotten her.

But she stayed strong. She never stopped believing. She never stopped trusting in the God of Israel.

The reason we know this to be true is because her entire household was with her when every wall but hers fell flat. Everyone who belonged to her was saved because she trusted in the God of Israel. They were delivered because of her steadfastness to stand on what God had promised. They reaped the benefits of her faith because of her obedience to the promise God gave to her.

> Wait for ADONAI. Be strong, let your heart take
> courage, and wait for ADONAI. (Psalm 27:14)

God gave Rahab a promise, and she waited in confident expectation for that word to come to fruition in her life. She didn't back down. She didn't lose hope. Instead, she clung to the promise of God never letting go. It's important for us to understand that there is no expiration date where the promises of God are concerned. If God promised it, he will do it. He is faithful to complete that which he started. He will bring it to fruition. Rahab understood this, and therefore, she held on to the promise God gave her. She continued to trust him even when in the natural, it seemed as if she were forgotten.

So not only must we follow Joshua's example in seeing our fight from the victory, but we must also follow Rahab's example. We must earnestly wait for God's plan regarding us to develop. It must be his will, his way, always.

What Just Happened?

As our journey continues, we find that the invasion of Canaan was well under way. The walls of Jericho had not only been breached but had literally fallen down flat. The city had been defeated, the inhabitants destroyed, with the only exception being Rahab and her entire household. They were saved and delivered by the promise of God.

The next objective in the path of conquest was the city of Ai. This city was situated east of Bethel, next to Beth-aven. Smaller than Jericho by far, its population was only about twelve thousand. However, even though it was smaller in size, it held great significant value. Its downfall would give Israel absolute control of the main route that ran through the central portion of the land of Canaan.

However, Ai also had some religious and historical significance. It was between Ai and Beth-El where God appeared to Abram, telling him that he was giving him this land.

> Then ADONAI appeared to Abram and said, "I will give this land to your seed." So, there he built an altar to ADONAI, who had appeared to him. From there he moved to the mountain to the east of Beth-El and erected his tent (with Beth-El to the west and Ai to the east). There he built an altar to ADONAI and called on the Name of ADONAI. (Genesis 12:7–8)

The promise that was given some four hundred years prior was now finding its fulfillment through the leadership of Joshua.

Using the same reconnaissance that was used in Jericho, Joshua sent out spies to infiltrate the city of Ai. Their mission was to spy out the land and bring back a report of their findings.

> Now Joshua sent men from Jericho to Ai, which is near Beth-aven, east of Bethel, and spoke to them saying: "Go up and spy out the land." So, the men went up and spied out Ai. When they returned to Joshua, they reported to him: "Let not all the people go up—only about two or three thousand men need go up and strike Ai, so don't wear out all the people there, for they are just a few. (Joshua 7:2–3)

The spies returned, telling Joshua that there was no need to send the entire army of Israel. Based on their findings, this would be a piece of cake. There were only a few of them. Israel could easily take them with only two to three thousand men.

Acting on their intel, Joshua chose three thousand soldiers from the armed forces of Israel and sent them off to defeat this small city.

In absolute confidence, the soldiers left the camp of Israel, only to encounter more than they bargained for. Their return was one of shame and utter defeat.

> So about 3,000 men from the people went up there, but they fled before the men of Ai. The men of Ai struck down about 36 of their men, and they chased them from outside the gate as far as Shebarim, striking them down on the slope. So, the hearts of the people melted and became like water. (Joshua 7:4–5)

This wasn't just a small defeat! The great and mighty were defeated by the small and puny. Israel had lost thirty-six of their men in this battle. Statistically speaking, that was a small number compared to the number of soldiers that went out. Out of the three thousand soldiers they had 2,964 return. However, these men who lost their lives, they weren't just strangers or acquaintances. They were family members—husbands, brothers, uncles, and cousins. Their lives mattered. Everyone in camp would feel this tremendous loss, especially Joshua, the man responsible for sending those men into that battle. To say that this defeat rocked Joshua to the core would be an understatement.

> Joshua then tore his clothes and fell to the ground on his face before the ark of ADONAI until evening, both he and the elders of Israel, and they put dust on their heads. "Alas, ADONAI Elohim [LORD God]!" Joshua said, "Why did You ever bring this people across the Jordan? Is it to deliver us into the hand of the Amorites—to destroy us? If only we had been content and dwelled beyond the Jordan. (Joshua 7:6–7)

Joshua's reaction upon hearing this news was to immediately fall on his face before God, which brings us to the next Life Lesson that we can glean through Joshua, and that is this: *God should always be your* go-to *person*. It is not your friend, not your spouse, not your brother or sister, mother or father but God! He is to be your go to person—always.

Joshua poured his heart out to God. He didn't mince words. He didn't sugarcoat his feelings. In fact, it's interesting how very similar Joshua's words are to that of the Israelites while wandering the desert.

Joshua asked God, "Why did you ever bring this people across the Jordan? Is it to deliver us into the hand of the Amorites—to destroy us? If only we had been content and dwelled beyond the Jordan!"

In their wilderness experience, the Israelites were constantly saying they should have just stayed in Egypt—they were so much better off there—which, mind you, had infuriated both Caleb and Joshua when giving their report of the Promised Land.

Yet here, we have Joshua pretty much saying the same thing—if we had stayed beyond the Jordan, we would have been so much better off. We then see a small glimpse into the heart of Joshua that we hadn't seen before.

> Oh, my Lord, what can I say, now that Israel has turned its back before its enemies? For when the Canaanites and all the inhabitants of the land hear of it, they will surround us and cut off our name from the earth. Then what will You do for Your great Name? (Joshua 7:8–9)

Joshua's concern here was what others thought of him. They turned back. They ran away. What were their enemies going to think? Notice that Joshua said "Our name will be cut off!" In other words, their reputation would be ruined because of this.

We've all been there. We've all done that. Things don't play out according to what and how we think they should have, and we have the tendency to make it about us.

The important Life Lesson that we can learn from this is that *it's not about you; stop and look at the bigger picture.*

We have the tendency to make it about us when it's not, and we make it about others when it's really about us. So we need to *stop!* Have that selah moment and just ask God, "What am I missing here?"

Now was it wrong for Joshua to pour out his heart before God? No, absolutely *no.* The truth of the matter is this, God already knows what's in your heart. He already knows what you're thinking. So let your conversation be with him, allowing him to deal with the issues his way. The thing to remember about conversing with God is that it's not just about you spouting off and dumping everything on God. Conversing with God also entails paying close attention to his response.

> Then ADONAI said to Joshua, "Arise! Why are you fallen on your face? Israel has sinned. (Joshua 7:10–11a)

Wait! What? Let's just stop here and take a selah moment. If this were a TV show that we were watching, this would be the place where the scene would freeze, fade out, and the words showing on the scene would read "Ten Days Earlier."

The show would then begin again, and you would see the circumstances that brought you up to that point.

So let's pause in our story here and go back several days to the day Joshua relayed God's instructions concerning the invasion of Jericho.

> Joshua ordered the people, "Shout! For ADONAI has given you the city! But the city will be under the ban of destruction—it and all that is in it belong to ADONAI. Only Rahab the harlot will live, she and all who are with her in the house, because she hid the scouts that we sent. But you, just keep yourselves from the things under the ban. Otherwise you would make yourselves accursed by taking of the things under the ban, and so you would make the camp of Israel accursed and bring trouble on it. All the silver and gold and vessels of bronze and iron are holy to ADONAI, and must go into the treasury of ADONAI. (Joshua 6:16b–19)

God gave the Israelites a specific word concerning the spoils of the land. The city of Jericho was under the ban of destruction. This phrase "ban of destruction" is derived from the Hebrew word *herem*.[21] This is a word that has a complete opposite. In other words, it's like a two-sided coin.

The one side would represent that which is holy and clean, whereas the other side represents that which is profane and unclean. In essence, herem, as it pertains to the holy and clean, is to be devoted to God. Whereas, the other side of the coin, if you would, that which pertains to the profane and unclean, is reserved for destruction.

The heart of herem is God's exclusive ownership, an ownership not subject to redemption. It belongs to God, period. It is either devoted for destruction or devoted to God for his use only. To take herem (*something holy and solely devoted to God*) would make Israel itself herem (*profane and unclean before God*). Thus, bringing trouble upon them.

This wasn't a new concept for the children of Israel. In Deuteronomy, chapter 7, Moses told the children of Israel that when God brings them into the land that he has promised to give them and delivers the nations into their hands, they were to strike them down, utterly destroying them. They were instructed to tear down their altars, smash their pillars, cut down their Asherah poles and burn their carved images with fire. The cattle, the livestock, and the people were also under the ban of destruction—herem. God flat out told them if they did not destroy them, the inhabitants of the land would turn their hearts from following after ADONAI.

Scripture teaches us that the land of Canaan consisted of seven nations mightier than Israel. All seven nations were under the ban of destruction. However, out of those seven nations that they were to conquer, the children of Israel were allowed to keep the spoils from all the cities except one.

The first city, everything in it was herem. They were to destroy people and livestock, and they were to devote the spoils of the land to God. This city, and everything in it, was herem—it belonged to God.

For Israel to break herem (to keep rather than to devote) is tantamount to robbing God. Scripture speaks of this very thing through the words of the prophet Malachi.

> Will a man rob God? For you are robbing Me!"
> But you say: "How have we robbed You?" In the
> tithe and the offering. (Malachi 3:8)

There were seven nations within the Promised land, nations that were comprised of many cities. Now out of all those cities, only one was wholly devoted to God—Jericho, the firstfruits of their victories. That belonged to God. They could confiscate and keep for themselves the spoils of all the remaining cities, but Jericho was God's. It would be considered the tithe from the Promised Land. The silver, the gold, all the metals from Jericho belonged to God and were to go into the treasury of God. They were to be used for his holy purposes.

The last verse in Joshua, chapter 6, reads, "So ADONAI was with Joshua, and his fame was throughout the region."

Yet the first verse in Joshua, chapter 7, begins with "But Bnei-Yisrael unfaithfully violated the ban."

The distance between victory and defeat is oftentimes just one step, and more times than not, it is a step in the wrong direction.

> But Bnei-Yisrael unfaithfully violated the ban.
> Achan son of Carmi son of Zabdi son of Serah,
> of the tribe of Judah, took some of the banned
> things. So ADONAI's anger burned against Bnei-
> Yisrael. (Joshua 7:1)

The word *unfaithfully* comes from the Hebrew word *ma'hal*, and it means "a treacherous act, a betrayal of trust, a violation of allegiance and an act of treason."[22]

Achan committed a treacherous act against God by taking that which was holy and devoted to God and keeping it for his own purposes.

One of the things I want to bring your attention to is this, Achan was the one who sinned, and yet his sin affected the entire camp of Israel. You see, the effects of sin are comparable to the effects of a landmine—it is far reaching and touches those in close proximity. This brings us to the next Life Lesson we can learn from Joshua, and that is this: *sin is like a landmine—it affects everyone around you.*

Achan was the one who sinned. He was the only one who had taken what was holy and devoted to God for himself. Yet his sin affected the whole camp.

Consider this for a moment; if Joshua had had a conversation with God before attacking Ai rather than afterward, things would probably have played out a lot differently for Israel.

Oftentimes, when we have just experienced a victory in our lives, the tendency is to just keep moving forward in the momentum of that victory. However, if we are not careful, that momentum can cause us to miss out on a much-needed conversation with God. These conversations with God can, and oftentimes will, prevent undesirable outcomes from happening. This brings us to our next Life Lesson: *Don't stop asking. Don't stop seeking.*

The minute you stop asking God what you should do, in that second when you stop seeking his direction, that is the exact moment when the very momentum that propelled you to victory will send you spiraling into defeat. It is in the aftermath of a victory that we need to be even more attuned to the voice of God.

If Joshua had stopped and conversed with God regarding the next step as pertaining to Ai, God would have told him flat up—Israel sinned.

> Then ADONAI said to Joshua, "Arise! Why are you fallen on your face? Israel has sinned. Yes, they have also transgressed My covenant, which I commanded them. Now they have even taken of the things under the ban of destruction. So, they have also stolen and even deceived, and even put them among their own possessions. So Bnei-Yisrael cannot stand before their enemies. So, they turn their necks before their enemies, because they have come under the ban. I will not be with you any more unless you destroy whatever is under the ban from among you. (Joshua 7:10–12)

You cannot stand against the enemy when you are standing against God. Remember, God always stands on the side of *righteousness*. Therefore, when you enter into sin, you are on the opposite side of *righteousness*. No longer standing beside God, you are now standing in direct opposition to God. Yet even in the midst of their sin, God's grace is extended to the children of Israel.

> Arise! Consecrate the people and say, "Consecrate yourselves for tomorrow, for thus says ADONAI, the God of Israel: Something under the ban is in the midst of you, Israel. You will not be able to stand up before your enemies until you remove whatever is under the ban from among you." (Joshua 7:13)

God was not going to bring his judgment until the morning of the next day. Thereby, giving Achan one more chance to repent of his sin before it was too late. Who knows, God may have relented if Achan had only repented. God's desire is for mercy rather than judgment. We see a perfect example of this mercy triumphing over judgment in the book of Jonah.

> When the word reached the king of Nineveh, he rose from his throne, took off his robe, covered himself in sackcloth, and sat in the ashes. He made a proclamation saying: "In Nineveh, by the decree of the king and his nobles, no man or beast, herd or flock, may taste anything. They must not graze nor drink water. But cover man and beast with sackcloth. Let them cry out to God with urgency. Let each one turn from his evil way and from the violence in his hands. Who knows? God may turn and relent, and turn back from his burning anger, so that we may not perish." When God saw their deeds—that they turned from their wicked ways—God relented from the calamity that He said He would do to them, and did not do it. (Jonah 3:6–10)

However, Achan didn't repent. Nor did he come forward. He didn't relinquish what rightfully belonged to God but held onto it instead. For what purpose? Did he honestly think that God didn't know what he did? His actions attested to that very thing.

Achan had all night to think about what he did. Even in the morning, as Joshua began to call each tribe to stand before him, he had time to voluntarily repent.

Scripture tells us the process for revealing who had sinned. Each tribe would be called forward. From within that tribe, the various clans would then step forward. Of those clans, family by family would step forward. When a family was chosen, man by man would step forward. During that entire process, Achan refused to take ownership of his sin.

> Then he brought forward the clans of Judah, and He took the family of the Zerahites. Then he brought forward the family of Zerahites man by man, and Zabdi was taken. Then he brought forward his household man by man, and Achan son of Carmi son of Zabdi son of Zerah of the tribe of Judah was taken. So, Joshua said to Achan, "My son, give glory now to ADONAI, God of Israel, and give praise to Him, and confess to me now what you have done—hide nothing from me. (Joshua 7:17–18)

Once Achan's sin had been revealed, Joshua told him to give glory to ADONAI and to praise him. Earlier in this chapter, we learned that Achan had acted unfaithfully toward God, causing his anger to burn toward Israel. This act of unfaithfulness was an act of treason. It was a betrayal of trust and a violation of allegiance. The items that Achan stole were items that belonged to God. In essence, it was the tithe of Jericho.

Our giving that which is devoted to God, to God, that is an act of worship. Whether it is the giving of the tithe or the giving of offerings, it is an act of worship. When we hold back what is rightfully God's, we are denying him of the worship he deserves and are committing an unfaithful, treacherous act against God.

Joshua was giving Achan the opportunity to give God the worship Achan's sin had denied him. Yet in Achan's confession to Joshua

LIFE LESSONS & SELAH MOMENTS

explaining what he did, you can almost hear the desire in his voice as he described what he stole.

> When I saw among the spoil a beautiful Shinar mantle and 200 shekels of silver and a wedge of gold 50 shekels in weight, I coveted them and took them. (Joshua 7:21a)

There are two words that I want to draw your attention to. The first word is *saw* which means "to look at, observe, consider and give attention to."[23] The second word is *coveted* which means "to lust after."[24]

This wasn't just a casual glance that Achan gave to these items. He didn't just see them out of the corner of his eye. He looked at them. He turned his attention toward them. He considered them. In other words, he thought about it good and hard, and the more he thought about it, the more he lusted after it.

What he did wasn't just a spontaneous action without thought and awareness. He was intentional in his actions. He saw it, he coveted it, and he took it.

We see this progression of sin broken down for us in James's letter to the twelve tribes in the dispersion.

> Let no one say when he is tempted, "I am being tempted by God:—for God cannot be tempted by evil, and He himself tempts no one. But each one is tempted when he is dragged away and enticed by his own desire. Then when desire has conceived, it gives birth to sin, and when sin is full grown, it brings forth death. (James 1:13–15)

The first item that Achan mentioned is the beautiful Shinar mantle. The name Shinar occurs eight times in the Hebrew Scriptures, and in every occurrence it refers to Babylonia.[25]

The next word I want to draw your attention to is the word *mantle* which comes from the Hebrew word *addereth*. This means "prophet's garment and glory."[26]

This mantle identified to whom you belonged. It was a Babylonian mantle worn by a false prophet who gave glory to a false god. In essence, Achan exchanged God's glory for the glory of a false god.

Not only did Achan deny God the worship due him, but by stealing that Shinar mantle, he willingly aligned his allegiance with that of a false god.

In spite of the fact that Achan admitted his sin, his heart was still connected to these items. There was no true repentance on his part. Therefore, there was no mercy or forgiveness extended. This brings us to the next Life Lesson in this journey with Joshua, and that is this: *whatever has your focus has you.*

Achan's focus had shifted. He had taken his eyes off of the God of Abraham, Isaac, and Jacob. God's instruction that was to be uppermost in his heart and mind was slowly drowned out by the whisperings of an invisible enemy.

God, through the leadership of Joshua, had instructed the children of Israel to be strong and resolute in their observance of his instructions. He even warned them not to become distracted but to keep their eyes fixed upon him.

> Only be strong, and resolute to observe diligently the Torah which Moses, My servant commanded you. Do not turn from it to the right or to the left, so you may be successful wherever you go. This book of the Torah should not depart from your mouth—you are to meditate on it day and night, so that you may be careful to do everything written in it. For then you will make your ways prosperous and then you will be successful. (Joshua 1:7–8)

Distractions, interruptions, commotions, disruptions—all attention-drawers, tools used by the enemy to cause you to not only lose your focus but your footing as well.

Second Chances

The tragic loss at Ai, where thirty-six men lost their lives, was a direct result of a defiant treacherous act that took place in Jericho. This wasn't a spontaneous action, without thought or intent. Under Achan's own admission, he saw the object of his desire and lusted after it. Despite all the warnings given before and during the battle of Jericho, he took that which was forbidden and then tried to hide his sin, thus, bringing upon himself and the nation the judgment of God.

This progression of sin is an exact replica of the pattern laid out before us in the actions of Adam and Eve.

> Now the woman saw that the tree was good for food, and that it was a thing of lust for the eyes, and that the tree was desirable for imparting wisdom. So, she took of its fruit and she ate. She also gave to her husband who was with her and he ate. Then the eyes of both of them were opened and they knew that they were naked; so, they sewed fig leaves together and made for themselves loin-coverings. And they heard the sound of ADONAI Elohim going to and from in the garden in the wind of the day. So, the man and his wife hid themselves from the presence of ADONAI Elohim in the midst of the Tree of the garden. (Genesis 3:6–8)

They, too, saw the object of their desire and lusted after it. They took it and then tried to hide their sin. Thus, bringing upon themselves and all mankind God's judgment.

Judgment and punishment came in the Garden of Eden; their sin brought death to all mankind.

We see that same scenario played out here in Achan's life. His choices, his decisions, his sin affected those around him. Judgment and punishment came in the city of Ai because of Achan's actions.

For just a moment, I want us to pause and take a selah moment. I want us to revisit some of the events of Jericho as they unfolded. Prior to taking the city, the children of Israel had all been informed of the ban of destruction. Jericho was under herem. The animals, as well as the people, were to be destroyed. The spoils of the land which consisted of the silver, gold, and precious metals were to be devoted for God's use only.

The shofarot had blown. The shout had sounded. The walls had fallen down. The armed forces of Israel had entered the city of Jericho, killing every living thing.

With the dust settling, man, woman, and child could be seen going through the city collecting the spoils of the land for God. It would be safe to surmise that Joshua, as their leader, would be going through the city, calling out and reminding the people of God's command.

> All the silver and gold and vessels of bronze and iron are holy to ADONAI, and must go into the treasury of ADONAI. (Joshua 6:19)

With this in mind, Achan's actions perfectly demonstrate the pattern of temptation. Temptation, when left unchecked, will give birth to sin, and unrepentant sin always leads to death.

Achan had so many opportunities to repent. He had all night to think about his actions and to turn his heart back to God. In the morning, God gave him additional time as each tribe was called forward to see if they would be the one God would point out to Joshua. When the Tribe of Judah was chosen, Achan still had time to confess his sin as clan after clan stepped forward, only to be exonerated by God.

When the clan of the Zerahites was chosen, Achan still had time to come forward as the head of each household stepped forward. Even after Achan's father's household was chosen, he still had time to repent as brother after brother stepped forward, only to be cleared of all guilt. Yet he still remained silent, until God finally pointed him out to Joshua.

> So, Joshua said to Achan, "My son, give glory now to ADONAI, God of Israel, and give praise to Him, and confess to me now what you have done—hide nothing from me. (Joshua 7:19)

Achan's heart was so hardened through the deceitfulness of sin that it wasn't until Joshua confronted him that he finally acknowledged his sin. This brings us to the next Life Lesson that we can learn from Joshua, and that is this: *the acknowledgment of sin is not equivalent to the repentance of sin.*

Achan might have acknowledged his sin, but he didn't repent. Yet even here, we see God's merciful grace in Joshua's response when confronting Achan. We can't forget that Achan caused the death of thirty-six brave, dedicated men under Joshua's leadership. He was a thief, a murderer, and a fool. Yet Joshua didn't call him by any of those names. He called him son. He didn't disown him because of his sin. He wanted Achan to make a repentant confession so he could extend mercy rather than judgment. In essence, Joshua wanted to save him rather than condemn him, but the outcome would lie in the response of Achan's heart.

You see, God doesn't want his last word to be one of judgment but rather one of mercy. We see that in his words to the prophet Ezekiel.

> Do I delight at all in the death of the wicked? It is a declaration of ADONAI. Rather, should he not return from his ways, and live? But when the righteous turns away from his righteousness, and commits iniquity and does according to all the

detestable acts that the wicked man does, will he live? None of his righteous deeds that he has done will be remembered; for his trespass that he trespassed and for his sin that he has sinned, for them he will die. (Ezekiel 18:23–24)

But when the wicked man turns away from his wickedness that he committed and does what is lawful and right, his soul will live. Because he considers and turns away from all his transgressions that he committed, he will surely live, not die. (Ezekiel 18:27–28)

Cast off from you all your transgressions that you have committed. Make yourselves a new heart and a new spirit. Why will you die, house of Israel? For I have no pleasure in the death of anyone who dies—it is a declaration of ADONAI—so return, and live! (Ezekiel 18:31–32)

God's heart is for us to truly repent so that he can relent from the judgment that we so rightfully deserve. We actually see that very thing demonstrated in the stunning reversal of the fates of the Israelite Achan and the Canaanite Rahab.

Achan, heir to a renowned Israelite family line, suffered the fate of Canaanite Jericho, while Rahab—as Canaanite as they come—escaped it.

Rahab, the ultimate "outsider," became an "insider" in Israel by submitting to ADONAI's authority, while Achan, "the exemplary insider," made himself an "outsider" by rejecting God's authority. The result of Rahab's submissive obedience was forgiveness, while Achan's blatant rebellion and lack of repentance received judgment.

Achan may have acknowledged his sin, but there was not a repentant confession of that sin. His greed brought trouble upon his entire house. King Solomon attests to this very truth when he wrote, "One greedy for gain troubles his household."[27]

Then Joshua, and all Israel with him, took Achan son of Zerah, the silver, the mantle, the wedge of gold, his sons, his daughters, his oxen, his donkeys, his sheep and his tent, and all that he had, and they brought them up to the Valley of Achor. Then Joshua said, "Why have you brought trouble on us? ADONAI will trouble you this day." Then all Israel stoned him with stones, burned them with fire and stoned them with stones. They raised over him a great heap of stones that stands to this day. Then ADONAI turned from the fierceness of His anger. Therefore, the name of that place has been called the Valley of Achor to this day. (Joshua 7:24–26)

Achan and all that belonged to him were taken outside the camp of Israel to the Valley of Achor. This word *Achor* means "trouble or disturbance."[28]

For after all, it is right in the sight of God to pay back trouble to those who trouble you. (2 Thessalonians 1:6)

Achan was taken outside the camp so that the camp that was troubled or disturbed by his sin might not be defiled by his death.

The contrast between the actions of Rahab the Canaanite and Achan the Israelite are striking. Rahab's obedience to the God of Israel saved her and her entire household. Whereas, Achan's disobedience caused the death of not only himself but his entire household. In Rahab's situation, we see the extent of God's mercy. In Achan's situation, we see the extent of God's judgment. Sin was exposed. Judgment was served. We now see the fierceness of God's anger turning from Israel.

With Israel now in right standing with God, Joshua received the battle plan for attacking and defeating Ai.

> Then ADONAI said to Joshua, "Do not be afraid or
> dismayed. Take all the people of war with you and
> arise, go up to Ai. Behold, I have given the king
> of Ai, his people, his city and his land into your
> hand. Then you will do to Ai and its kings as you
> did to Jericho and its king—except you will take
> its spoil and its cattle as plunder for yourselves. Set
> an ambush for the city behind it. (Joshua 8:1–2)

The first thing God told Joshua was that he didn't have to be afraid. There was no need for him to worry. He then told Joshua that the entire army would be going to battle and not just a few like last time. It wasn't that they needed the entire army to defeat Ai—again, the battle belongs to the Lord. ADONAI sent the entire armed forces of Israel so that they could all share in the victory and, thus, restore their confidence in preparation for the battles yet to come.

Once again, God started off with a promise and then followed that promise with a set of instructions. They were to do to Ai what they did to Jericho, with one exception. They were to destroy all the people, but the livestock and the spoils were theirs to keep.

If only Achan had been patient and had not given into his greed. If he had but trusted God and his goodness, he would have gotten the desires of his heart the right way. Remember, it has to be God's will, his way, always.

The game plan that God revealed to Joshua was unlike any strategy of war that they had been a part of thus far. In fact, truth be told, every strategy God had given to Joshua had been altogether different than the strategies that Moses was given.

The children of Israel had experienced the effect of lifting the rod of Aaron up over the battlefield and the victory that ensued.

They had also witnessed the effect of the psychological warfare implemented when marching around the city of Jericho while continually blowing the shofarot.

Here, with the city of Ai, God began teaching them a new strategy. This strategy would involve a sneak attack through the means of an unexpected ambush.

Joshua, after receiving his orders from God, began to lay out the step-by-step process of this stealth attack. Three thousand soldiers would leave that night to secretly and stealthily make their way behind the city of Ai. They were to stay hidden until they received word to attack the city from behind.

Meanwhile, five thousand soldiers would go and station themselves between Bethel and Ai, which would be west of the city. If you'll remember, the place between Bethel and Ai was the very place God spoke to Abram, giving him the promise that this land was being given to him. It was at that location where Abram built an altar to ADONAI as a reminder of the promise God had given. Therefore, the ambush team lying in wait at that location would see that altar, recognizing what it represented, thus, reaffirming God's promise to them that he had given them the city.

The remaining army of soldiers would be with Joshua just north of the city, with the rear guard stationed west of Ai.

Instructions were given, and God's strategy of war was revealed. Everyone was to go to their respective places, fully understanding the role they would play in this attack. Lights. Camera. Action.

> Then Joshua rose up early in the morning and mustered the people. He and the elders of Israel marched before the people of Ai. (Joshua 8:10)

> So, it came to pass when the king of Ai saw this, the men of the city hurried and rose up early, and went out to meet Israel in battle, he and all his people at the appointed place facing the Arabah. But he did not know that there was an ambush against him behind the city. So, Joshua and all Israel pretended to be beaten before them and fled by the way of the wilderness. Then all the people who were in Ai were summoned to pursue them, so they pursued Joshua and were drawn away from the city. Not a man was left in Ai or Bethel who did not go out after Israel so they left the

> city open as they chased after Israel. Then ADONAI said to Joshua, "Stretch out the javelin that is in your hand toward Ai, for I will give it into your hand." So, Joshua stretched out the javelin that was in his hand toward the city. (Joshua 8:14–18)

God's plan was for Joshua to lead only a portion of the armed forces in what was to look like a replay of the first attack against Ai. However, this time, their luring of Ai's defenders from the city and pretending to retreat was a bait, a trap for Ai's soldiers. God's plan was to use the confidence buoyed by Ai's earlier victory to Israel's advantage.

Seeing only the attacking force of Joshua's soldiers, the defenders of Ai thought that the second battle would turn out like the first. They had no idea of the ambush that was behind the city or the ambushes west and north of the city that awaited them.

As the soldiers of Ai were running toward the retreating soldiers of Israel, God spoke to Joshua and told him to stretch out the javelin that was in his hand toward Ai, for God had given the city to him.

I want us to pause here and take a selah moment. Stop and think about the scene playing out before us. The soldiers of Israel had captured the attention of Ai. Ai's defenders left the city in hot pursuit of the now-retreating soldiers. Joshua's soldiers were waiting for the signal from the ambush team located behind Ai that the city had been taken captive. Until then, they were to retreat from the oncoming soldiers.

The signal they were waiting for would be the smoke rising from the burning city of Ai, confirmation that the city had been taken by the ambush team hiding behind the city.

It was at this point in their retreat that God spoke to Joshua and gave him a direct order. In order for Joshua to carry out this order, he would have to stop, turn around, and stretch out the javelin toward the city in obedience to God's word.

Many of us, when we think of the word *javelin*, automatically envision a spear. But the Hebrew word used here is *kiydown* which is a "short sword" whose primary use was to slice a person's throat.[29]

LIFE LESSONS & SELAH MOMENTS

> As soon as he stretched out his hand, the ambush
> arose quickly from their place, ran and entered
> the city and captured it; and immediately set the
> city on fire. (Joshua 8:19)

There was no way that those waiting in ambush behind the city would be able to see Joshua's signal to attack. Even if it was a spear, the city itself would have blocked them from seeing that spear raised. So how did they know when to attack?

> While we are fleeing before them, you will rise
> up from the ambush and take possession of the
> city, for ADONAI your God will give it into your
> hand. Now when you have seized the city, you
> will set the city on fire—according to the word of
> ADONAI you must do. See that you do as I have
> ordered you. (Joshua 8:6b–8)

The Commander of heaven's armies was on the battlefield that day. He was giving orders to Joshua and his men all throughout that battle. I believe that the order given to Joshua to lift up his javelin toward the city of Ai was almost immediately followed with God's command to attack the city from behind.

Once Joshua and his men saw the smoke rising from the burning city, his team quickly turned and attacked the soldiers pursuing them.

For just a moment, I want to redirect your attention to the words written in Joshua 8:17, which reads, "Not a man was left in Ai or Bethel who did not go out after Israel."

Not only was Ai defeated that day, but Bethel was defeated as well. Remember, there was a team of five thousand men hiding in ambush between Bethel and Ai. I would not be at all surprised to find that this team was made up of the 2,964 men who had returned defeated from the first attack on Ai. I believe this team was sent to that exact spot for two important reasons. First, being in that place, they would see the altar built by Abram, reminding them of the promise ADONAI had given them: "I am giving your seed this land."[30]

The second reason they were stationed there was God knew that the men of Bethel were in allegiance with Ai. When the soldiers from Bethel came out to fight with Ai against Israel, the armed forces of Israel were positioned to ambush them.

Ai and Bethel were both conquered by God's strategic plan of attack. After this great victory, we see Joshua fulfilling the command of God that had been spoken through Moses to the children of Israel.

> Now when ADONAI your God brings you into the land you are going to possess, you are to set the blessing on Mount Gerizim and the curse on Mount Ebal. Are they not across the Jordan toward the west, in the land of the Canaanites who dwell in the Arabah—opposite Gilgal, beside the oaks of Moreh? (Deuteronomy 11:29–30)

With both Bethel and Ai defeated, Israel now had full control of the main route that ran throughout the land of Canaan. For this reason, they were able to safely travel from Ai to Mount Ebal where Joshua carried out the command of ADONAI. At the place God designated, Joshua reminded God's people of the blessings and curses God had set before them.

If you obey, you will be blessed. If you refuse to obey, then all of these curses will be upon you. God's desire is for us to choose life, to choose the blessings associated with obedience.

Don't go the way of Achan. Don't lose your focus. Stop. Look and listen. The choice is yours. *Life, obedience, blessing, or…death, rebellion, curses*—which will you choose? Don't make the same mistake of Achan. Choose *life*. Choose obedience. Choose blessings.

Stop. Look. Listen.

Israel was moving forward in their conquest of the land. They had invaded and defeated Jericho, and in their second invasion of Ai, they had defeated it. They had just returned from Mount Ebal and Mount Gerizim where Joshua read the words of the Torah, both the blessing and the curse. In fact, there wasn't a word of all that Moses had commanded that Joshua did not read before the congregation of Israel.

Once again, their mission was clear. Their job was to conquer the land, ridding it of the Hittites, the Amorites, the Canaanites, the Perizzites, the Hivites and the Jebusites, just as ADONAI their God had commanded.

Word had quickly spread of Israel's latest failure and conquest of Ai. Israel now had control over the main route that ran through the central portion of the land of Canaan. They had to be stopped. A joining of forces had to be made.

> Now when all the kings who were west of the Jordan, in the hill country, in the lowland and along the shore of the Great Sea to the vicinity of Lebanon—the Hittites, the Amorites, the Canaanites, the Perizzites, the Hivites, and the Jebusites—heard about it, they gathered themselves together as a unified alliance to fight against Joshua and Israel. (Joshua 9:1–2)

Interestingly enough, their response over the defeat of Ai was totally different than their earlier response when Israel first entered their land.

> Now it came about when all the Amorite kings
> beyond the Jordan westward and all the Canaanite
> kings by the sea heard how ADONAI had dried
> up the waters of the Jordan before Bnei-Yisrael
> until they had crossed, their heart melted, nor
> was there any spirit in them anymore, because of
> Bnei-Yisrael. (Joshua 5:1)

However, after the defeat of Ai, their reaction was quite different. Their hearts weren't melting. The fight hadn't gone out of them. In fact, quite the opposite happened. All the kings joined together in an alliance for a full-out frontal attack against Joshua and Bnei-Yisrael.

So what changed? Could it be that they zeroed in on the defeat of Israel by the small and insignificant Ai, a city of only twelve thousand? Perhaps their reasoning was if they were once defeated by such a small army, then they could easily be defeated by a unified army comprised of the greatest warriors. Consequently, an alliance was made

However, there was one city that saw the futility of that reasoning. It wasn't Joshua and Bnei-Yisrael that they would be fighting against but the God of Joshua and Bnei-Yisrael. Therefore, they came up with a plan of their own.

> But when the inhabitants of Gibeon heard what
> Joshua had done to Jericho and Ai, they acted
> craftily. They went and traveled as ambassadors,
> took worn-out-sacks for their donkeys and worn-
> out wine skins, cracked and patched up, along
> with worn-out, patched up sandals on their feet
> and worn-out clothes on them. All the bread of
> their provision was dry and had become crumbly.
> Then they went to Joshua in the camp at Gilgal,
> and said to him and the men of Israel, "We have
> come from a far country. So now, make a trea-
> ty-covenant with us." (Joshua 9:3–6)

Gibeon was one of the larger cities in Canaan. In fact, it was one of the royal cities of Canaan. It was located in the central mountains about seven miles southwest from Ai and approximately nine miles northwest of Jerusalem. The men of Gibeon were described as being both courageous and mighty.

Yet they didn't join in the alliance of the kings but, rather, aligned themselves with three smaller towns. Chephirah was a small town situated eight to nine miles west of Gibeon. Beeroth was referred to as a "city of woods" and was located eight miles north of Jerusalem, twenty minutes outside of Gibeon. Then there was the city of Kiriath-jearim situated right next to Beeroth and referred to as the "city of forests."

This alignment wasn't to attack and defeat Israel but, rather, to trick Israel into making a peace treaty with them.

There are two different perspectives when viewing this passage. The first and most obvious perspective is that of the actions of Joshua and the children of Israel. The second perspective, one that is perhaps not as obvious, focuses our attention on the Gibeonites.

For just a moment, I want us to revisit the passage that Joshua would have read to the children of Israel when on Mount Ebal and Mount Gerizim after the defeat of Ai. Revisiting this passage will enable us to better understand the dilemma that Joshua and the children of Israel now faced.

> When you go near a city to fight against it, call out shalom to it. Now if it answers you shalom and opens up to you, then all the people found in it will serve you as forced laborers. If it does not make peace with you but makes war against you, then lay siege against that city. When ADONAI your God hands it over to you, you are to strike all its males with the sword. Only the women, children, livestock and all that is in the city—all its spoil—may you take as plunder for yourself. So, you may consume your enemies' spoil, which ADONAI your God has given you. Thus, you will

do to all the cities that are very distant from you, which are not among the towns of these nations nearby. However, only from the cities of these peoples, which ADONAI your God is giving you as an inheritance, you must not let anything that breathes live. You must utterly destroy them—the Hittites, the Amorites, the Canaanites, the Perizzites, the Hivites and the Jebusites—just as ADONAI your God has commanded you. (Deuteronomy 20:10–17)

Within this passage there are two directives given upon entering the Promised Land. The first one deals with all the cities that are far away, whereas the second one deals with all the cities that were close and nearby.

The cities that were distant and far away, Israel could offer them shalom. Accepting this offer would mean they would become Israel's servants, thus, making them servants of ADONAI. However, if they refused shalom, thus, refusing to become Israel's servants, all the men of that city would be killed. The women, children, and livestock would be considered the spoils of their victory.

Not so for those cities that were near to Israel. They were under herem—devoted for destruction. Nothing breathing was to live except for the livestock that would be considered the spoils of their victory.

It's interesting to note that when the Israelites were approached by these strangers from a distant land, their first instinct was to distrust them.

Then the men of Israel said to the Hivites: "Perhaps you are living among us. How then should we make a covenant with you?" (Joshua 9:7)

The men of Gibeon quickly responded by saying, "We are your servants." In other words, they were coming in shalom and were willing to become the servants of Israel, thus, making them the servants of ADONAI.

These words *shalom* and *servants* would have been familiar to the Israelites. More than likely, they would have triggered the memory of Joshua reading those very words from the Torah days before at Mount Ebal and Mount Gerizim.

At this point in our story, the Gibeonites began to tell Joshua their tale of traveling a great distance because of the Name of ADONAI, their God. They, too, had heard the stories of what God had done for them in Egypt. They had also heard what God did to the two Amorite kings, Sihon and Og. They admitted to Joshua and the children of Israel that it was because of ADONAI that they had traveled this great distance. Their purpose was for shalom, to become the servants of Israel.

They then proceeded to show Joshua proof of their long journey. Their bread that was once hot and fresh was now dry and crumbly. Their wineskins, which were new when they began their journey, were now cracked and weathered. Their garments and sandals which were once fresh and clean were now dirty and worn, all signs of their great journey, all signs that they were telling the truth.

For these reasons Joshua, along with the men of Israel, fell prey to their deception, which brings us to the next Life Lesson that we can learn from Joshua, and that is this: *learn the importance of taking a selah moment.*

Stop. Look. Listen. Stop what you're doing. Look to God and listen for the sound of his voice. Step back from the situation and have a conversation with God. You would think that this was a concept that Joshua would have learned by now, especially after what happened with Ai. His failure to stop and have a conversation with God concerning Ai caused them to move forward without God.

Yet aren't we all guilty of doing this? We know the importance of making divinely directed decisions and yet, more times than not, the decisions we make are anything but divinely directed. We look at the circumstance and then act. God wants us to look at the circumstance and turn *to him*.

Oftentimes, we base our decisions on what appears to be true rather than on the *truth* itself. The prophet Samuel was warned against doing this very thing when he was sent to anoint God's chosen king.

> But ADONAI said to Samuel, "Do not look at his appearance or his stature, because I have already refused him. For he does not see a man as man sees, for man looks at the outward appearance, but ADONAI looks into the heart. (1 Samuel 16:7)

Even Yeshua addresses the damage of putting your trust in what you see versus what you know to be true.

> For false messiahs and false prophets will rise up and show great signs and wonders so as to lead astray, if possible, even the chosen. (Matthew 24:24)

Scripture tells us that the men of Israel actually handled these items as well as looked them over. Because of their appearance, they made the decision to extend peace to the Gibeonites and to cut a covenant with them.

> So the men of Israel took some of the provisions, and did not seek counsel from ADONAI's mouth. So, Joshua made peace with them and cut a covenant with them, to let them live. (Joshua 9:14)

They failed to seek God's counsel and because of that, they were deceived.

> A discerning heart gains knowledge, the ear of the wise seeks knowledge. (Proverbs 18:15)

What if they would have stopped and simply taken a selah moment? If they would have simply asked God, he would have given them the necessary discernment to see through the appearance of truth to the reality of truth. This brings us to the next Life Lesson: *don't miss an opportunity to hear God speak.*

I want us to shift our focus now and give our attention to Gibeon. You see, in the midst of the lies, there was truth to be found. They did come to Joshua because of the Name of ADONAI. They had heard of God's exploits in Egypt as well as what he did to the two Amorite kings. That was all truth.

What they didn't disclose was that they had probably also heard of the events surrounding Jericho and Ai—especially the events of Jericho. They would have heard of the ban of destruction—the herem of Jericho—the complete annihilation of every breathing thing within that city with the one exception of Rahab and her family. She was spared. Her family was spared.

The question they must have been asking themselves was *why?* What did she do to cause ADONAI to spare her?

Let's pause here a moment and look at the similarities between Rahab and the Gibeonites. Rahab, like the Gibeonites, was a native of Canaan. The Gibeonites and Rahab both believed God was giving the land to Israel.

Joshua 2:9 reads, "and she said to the men: 'I know that ADONAI has given you the land.'" We see this same confidence in the Gibeonites' response to Joshua when asked why they deceived Israel.

> So, they answered Joshua and said: "It was because your servants were clearly told that ADONAI your God had commanded Moses to give you all the land and to destroy the inhabitants of the land before you. So, we were very afraid for our lives because of you, and so we did this. (Joshua 9:24)

Another similarity was that Rahab and the Gibeonites both responded with reverential fear before God's people, Israel. They were also alike in the fact that they both acted cunningly in order that they and their families might find refuge among the people of Israel. Just take a look at what the writer of the book of Hebrews has to say about Rahab.

By faith Rahab the prostitute did not perish with those who were disobedient, because she welcomed the spies with shalom. (Hebrews 11:31)

Do you remember the words that Joshua read at Mount Ebal? "Now if the city answers you with shalom and opens up to you, then all the people found in it will serve you."[31]

As quickly as word seemed to spread about what was happening in the camp of Israel, I would not be the least bit surprised to find that the Gibeonites had spies of their own. Nor would I be surprised to find that the idea of portraying themselves as one from a distant land came from eavesdropping at that mountain.

When you think about it, Rahab was under the ban of destruction, until she extended shalom to the spies, acknowledging the God of Israel. God spared her and her family because of her submission to his authority.

Gibeon was also under the ban of destruction, until they extended shalom to the people of God, becoming their servants.

What's so interesting in this story is that Joshua went into covenant with Gibeon, basing their decision on their appearances.

God doesn't see as man sees. He doesn't look at the outward appearance but at the heart. Which is exactly what he did with the Gibeonites. He looked at their heart and their willingness to submit themselves to his authority and leadership. You see, God doesn't want his final word to be judgment but, rather, redemption. This brings us to our next Life Lesson: *God always has the last word, but it's up to you whether that word will be one of judgment or mercy.*

Stop. Look. Listen. Take a selah moment and have a conversation with God. Don't let even one opportunity slip by where you could have had the chance to hear the voice of God speaking into your life. Remember, divinely directed decisions are almost always birthed out of selah moments.

The Battle Belongs to the Lord

Joshua and the children of Israel had been in the land of Canaan for a good while now. During this time, they had been made conquerors of Jericho through a miracle, victors over Ai by stratagem, and now masters of Gibeon through surrender. Having control of Ai and Bethel and now being in allegiance with Gibeon, the Israelites would have gained strategic control of all of central Canaan, including its major roads. It was because of this that Israel could now easily maneuver throughout the entire land of Canaan unencumbered.

The fall of Jericho, Ai, and Bethel had proven that Israel was bent on conquest. However, this unexpected peace treaty between the royal city of Gibeon and Israel had struck fear deep within the heart of Jerusalem's Amorite king, Adoni-zedek.

We know from Scripture that all the kings who were west of the Jordan, upon hearing the news of Ai's capture and defeat, had come together in a unified alliance to fight against Joshua and Israel. But now this had happened, an alliance with one of their own royal cities, a city far larger than Ai, whose men were strong and mighty, warriors that should have been, by all rights, fighting alongside King Adoni-zedek and not Joshua.

> Now it came to pass that Adoni-zedek king of Jerusalem heard that Joshua had taken Ai, and had utterly destroyed it—just as he had done to Jericho and its king, so he had done to Ai and its king—and that the inhabitants of Gibeon had made peace with Israel and remained among them. So, he feared greatly, because Gibeon was a large city, as one of the royal cities—in fact,

larger than Ai—and all its men were mighty. Therefore Adoni-zedek king of Jerusalem sent word to Hoham king of Hebron, Piram king of Jarmuth, Japhia king of Lachis and Debir king of Eglon saying: "Come up and help me! Let's attack Gibeon, for it has made peace with Joshua and Bnei-Yisrael." (Joshua 10:1–4)

Throughout the entire land of Canaan, stories of ADONAI and his exploits were being proclaimed. Reports of all that he had accomplished in Egypt through the ten plagues and the splitting of the Red Sea were heard everywhere. The most disturbing of these stories being told was about the deaths of the two Amorites kings who were beyond the Jordan—King Sihon of Heshbon and King Og of Bashan, who was at Ashtaroth.

These stories had reached yet another Amorite king, who had now become fearful for his life and kingdom. Upon hearing these reports, he sent word to the other Amorite kings to join forces with him to wage war against Gibeon. They would attack Gibeon, forcing them back under their allegiance. They had no intentions at this time to fight Israel. They wanted Gibeon back under their control. Five armies encamped around the city of Gibeon should knock some sense into them. They would either break their treaty with Israel or bear the consequences of their actions.

So, the five kings of the Amorites—the king of Jerusalem, the king of Hebron, the king of Jarmuth, the king of Lachish, and the king of Eglon—gathered themselves and went up, they and all their armies, camped against Gibeon and attacked it. Then the men of Gibeon sent word to Joshua in camp at Gilgal saying, "Don't abandon your servants! Come up to us quickly and save us! Help us, for all the kings of the Amorites living in the hill country have gathered against us." (Joshua 10:5–7)

With the city fully surrounded, somehow Gibeon managed to send word to Joshua of their situation. As you are imagining the scene before you, keep in mind that they didn't have phones, emails, or text messaging capabilities. What they did have at their disposal were feet, and they used them.

Trusted men from Gibeon would have had to sneak past the siege surrounding their city. Once they got past the troops, they would need to travel approximately forty-two kilometers or twenty-six miles on foot to Gilgal. At a leisure pace, this would take between eight to nine hours on foot. Running at a swift clip, it would probably have taken them between six to seven hours, give or take a few. The only thing going for them was that it was downhill all the way. These messengers would have reached Gilgal probably in the early evening hours. They got word to Joshua of their plight, and Joshua didn't even hesitate. He immediately left with the armed forces of Israel.

> So Joshua went up from Gilgal, he and all the
> people of war with him and all the mighty men
> of valor. (Joshua 10:7)

I want to pause here for just a moment. It's interesting to note that from the time that ADONAI spoke to Joshua during the battle of Ai up until this point, there had been no recorded conversations between Joshua and ADONAI. The last recorded conversation we have was when ADONAI told Joshua to point his javelin toward the city of Ai, signifying its downfall and Israel's victory.

For just a moment, I want you to think back on the encounter between Joshua and the Gibeonites. If you'll recall, Gibeon pretended to be from a distant country in order to align themselves with Israel. During that whole interchange, Israel never once spoke with God. They failed to seek counsel from God's mouth and, therefore, entered into a covenant under false pretenses. Interestingly enough, we have not heard one word from God concerning this whole Gibeon-Israelite peace treaty. The last time God was silent was during the first invasion of Ai. It wasn't until Joshua sought God that

God spoke, which actually brings us to the next Life Lesson, and that is this: *if you want God to open his mouth, then you must open his Word.*

Take that selah moment and seek God. Stop and have a conversation with him regarding your present circumstances. One way that we can do this is by getting into his word.

> Call to Me, and I will answer you—I will tell you
> great and hidden things, which you do not know.
> (Jeremiah 33:3)

That is exactly what God did for them at Ai. They asked, and he answered.

The circumstances surrounding the first invasion of Ai was that the Israelites had unknowingly broken herem as pertaining to Jericho. Once again, they had unknowingly broken herem, only this time as pertaining to Gibeon. Yet we still don't hear of a conversation between Joshua and God, even when the error of their ways had been revealed to them.

So you can just imagine the anxiety that must have been in the heart of Joshua upon hearing the news of Gibeon being under attack. By all rights, Joshua and Bnei-Yisrael were to have been the ones leading that attack and destroying the Gibeonites. However, they now find themselves on the side of the Gibeonites being their protectors.

You have to wonder if the question that Joshua once asked ADONAI wasn't running through his mind at that moment: "Are you on our side or on the side of our enemies?"[32]

This situation was filled with a bit of ambiguity here. At one time, the Gibeonites were considered their enemies, but now they were their allies.

If you'll remember, the answer to that question was that God never chooses sides. He is always on the side of righteousness. The right thing, the honorable thing for Joshua to do was to honor the vow that he made. Regardless of whether he was duped or not, they came to him in peace, seeking alignment with Israel and the God of Israel.

And it will come to pass that before they call, I
will answer, and while they are still speaking, I
will hear. (Isaiah 65:24)

Joshua made his decision. He chose to stand on the side of righteousness. It was at that moment of decision that God broke his
silence.

So, Joshua went up from Gilgal, he and all the
people of war with him and all the mighty men of
valor. ADONAI said to Joshua, "Do not fear them,
for I have given them into your hand. Not one of
them will stand before you. (Joshua 10:7–8)

In that moment, ADONAI reiterated the promise that he made
to Joshua east of the Jordan.

- You have nothing to fear.
- I am with you.
- I have given them into your hand.
- Not one of them will stand before you.

God spoke to Joshua, echoing the very words he gave to him
prior to their even entering Canaan.

No one will be able to stand before you all the
days of your life. Just as I was with Moses, so I
will be with you. I will not fail you or forsake you.
Chazak! Be strong! For you will lead these people to inherit the land I swore to their fathers to
give them. Have I not commanded you? Chazak!
Be strong! Do not be terrified or dismayed, for
ADONAI your God is with you wherever you go.
(Joshua 1:5–6, 9)

God was with them. Joshua and Bnei-Yisrael were standing on the side of righteousness, right next to their God. It was because of their covenant with ADONAI that God would honor the Gibeonite covenant.

The book of Job helps us to have a better understanding of this concept as it sheds more light into the power behind keeping covenant.

> Surely then Shaddai [*the Almighty*] will be your delight and you will lift up your face to God. You will pray to Him and He will hear you, and you will fulfill your vows. What you decide will be done, and light will shine on your ways. When people are brought low, and you say, "Lift them up!" then He will save the downcast. He will deliver even one who is not innocent, who will be delivered by the cleanness of your hands. (Job 22:26–30)

Pray to him, and he will hear you. Keep your vows or commitments, and he will save those who are hurting and in need. God has even promised to deliver those who aren't in right standing with him, simply based on your relationship with God.

We see what the Gibeonites did as deceptive and misleading, but God saw beyond that. He zeroed in on the heart of the matter. They came to Israel *because of* the Name of ADONAI. Their surrender to Israel was, in essence, a surrender to the God of Israel. They were now God's servants under his covering. For this reason, God gave his blessing to Joshua, reminding him of the promise he made, once again, confirming that God was with them, and no one would be able to stand against them.

With confidence, Joshua led the armed forces of Israel as they traveled uphill the twenty-six miles to Gibeon. Keep in mind, it would have taken them at a fast clip going uphill approximately seven to eight hours.

When they finally did reach the city of Gibeon, they saw that it was surrounded by the armies of those five Amorite kings, kings who never expected Israel to show up on the scene. They never expected Joshua and his army to come to the defense of the Hivites—treaty or no treaty. In fact, they were shocked when the army of Israel showed up.

> So Joshua came upon them suddenly by marching all night from Gilgal. (Joshua 10:9)

The armed forces of Israel showing up to defend Gibeon was the furthest thing from King Adoni-zedek's mind. He probably assumed, since Joshua was deceived into making a treaty with the Gibeonites in the first place, that the Israelites wouldn't feel the need to come to their rescue. Seeing them was an absolute shock. But what happened next sent them into absolute panic.

> ADONAI threw them into confusion before Israel, defeated them with a crushing defeat at Gibeon, chased them by the road that goes up to Beth-horon, and struck them as far as Azekah and Makkedah. While they were fleeing before Israel down the descent of Beth-horon, ADONAI cast down great stones from heaven on them all the way to Azekah so they died—more of them died from the hailstones than those Bnei-Yisrael killed with the sword. (Joshua 10:10–11)

What we see happening next is ADONAI-Tzva'ot stepping in to defend the Gibeonites. Scripture tells us that God threw them into confusion. The word *confusion* comes from the Hebrew word *hamam*, and it means "to move noisily, to make noise, to cause great difficulty and trouble, to confuse.""[33]

According to *Webster's Dictionary*, the word *confuse* means "to fail to differentiate one person from another."[34]

God moved noisily through those troops, defeating them with a crushing defeat. It was ADONAI who threw them into confusion. It was ADONAI who defeated them. It was ADONAI who chased them and struck them down.

Now if that wasn't enough, it says that as they were trying to get away, that ADONAI began casting down great stones from heaven on top of them. More of them died from the hailstones than those Bnei-Yisrael killed with the sword.

I want us to pause here and just think about this scene. The Amorite armies were taken by surprise by the arrival of Israel. Suddenly, a tremendous noise was heard moving through their ranks. This deafening roar caused both panic and confusion among the enemy soldiers. They couldn't tell who were fighting with them or against them, thus, causing them to turn on each other in fear and utter confusion.

King David describes a perfect picture of God coming down and doing battle on his behalf.

> In my distress I called on ADONAI, and cried to my God for help. From His Temple He heard my voice, my cry before Him came into His ears. Then the earth rocked and quaked. The foundations of mountains trembled. They reeled because He was angry. Smoke rose from His nostrils and consuming fire from His mouth. Coals blazed from Him. He parted the heavens and came down, with thick darkness under his feet. He rode upon a cheruv [*storm*] and flew. He soared on the wings of the wind. He made darkness His cover, His sukkah [*booth, tabernacle*] all around Him—dark waters, thick clouds. ADONAI also thundered in the heavens, and *Elyon* [*Almighty, Most High*] gave forth His voice, hail and fiery coals. He shot His arrows and scattered them, hurled lightning bolts and routed them. (Psalm 18:7–16)

What a perfect portrayal of God coming to their rescue. Think about it. In the midst of hurling those huge hailstones from the sky, not one of them missed their mark, huge hailstones falling from the sky, striking and killing only the enemies of Israel. That in and of itself was a miracle. Not one Israelite or Gibeonite, for that matter, was struck by the stones of heaven, which brings us to the next Life Lesson, and that is this: *God is your covering. Whatever comes at you, you are safely hidden under his wings.*

The writer of psalms speaks about this covering that you and I are safely hidden under.

> He will cover you with His feathers, and under His wings you will find refuge. His faithfulness is body armor and shield. A thousand may fall at your side, and ten thousand at your right hand, but it will not come near you. (Psalm 91:4, 7)

Joshua, chapter 10, is an amazing portrayal of the promise that the battle belongs to the Lord. We may be fighting in it, as Joshua and the children of Israel were, but the battle belongs to him.

This wasn't a quick battle. In fact, it had been going on all day, and now the sun was about to set. The faith that Joshua exhibited next is amazing. In the midst of this incredible battle, Joshua stopped and had a conversation with God, which actually brings us to our next Life Lesson: *now is a good time to talk with God*

You are never too busy to stop and have a conversation with God. Oftentimes, you will find that it isn't in the midst of our battles where we forget that *now is a good time to talk with God.* It's in those times of peace where our conversation seems to lag.

In the midst of all that activity, Joshua took a selah moment and had a conversation with God. It was in the middle of that conversation where Joshua told the *sun* to stand still and the *moon* to move over. And God made it happen.

> Then Joshua spoke to ADONAI, on the day ADONAI gave the Amorites over to Bnei-Yisrael, and said

> in the eyes of Israel: "Sun, stand still over Gibeon,
> Moon, move over the Aijalon Valley!" So, the sun
> stood still and the moon stopped until the nation
> took vengeance on its enemies. (Is it not written
> in the Book of Jashar?) Thus, the sun halted in
> the middle of the sky, and did not hurry to go
> down for about a full day. (Joshua 10:12–13)

Joshua had marched all night, and he had fought all day. One might expect that he would take a breather, get some rest, and hit it fresh again in the morning. But he didn't. Instead, he wished for the day to be prolonged so he could utterly and completely finish the task set before him.

> So it was that Joshua and Bnei-Yisrael finished
> striking them with a very great slaughter until
> they were wiped out, though some of their sur-
> vivors escaped into the fortified cities. Then all
> the people returned safely to Joshua in the camp
> at Makkedah. No one dared sharpen his tongue
> against Bnei-Yisrael. (Joshua 10:20–21)

The Israelites experienced an amazing victory. They saw first-hand God fighting for them—and not just for them but for Gibeon as well. They heard the audacious prayer of Joshua and saw God graciously grant him his request. They experienced God's strength flowing through them as they continued to fight and overcome the enemy.

We mustn't forget that they had traveled all night in order to reach Gibeon by morning. Immediately going into battle mode, they had fought all day. With God extending the day, they were given another twenty-four hours. In essence, they had been up for seventy-two hours and fighting for approximately forty-eight hours, all without rest. God was indeed their strength.

Now Joshua gave them a visual representation of the victory that God had in store for them down the road.

> When they brought out those kings to Joshua, Joshua summoned all the men of Israel and said to the chiefs of the men of war who had gone with him, "Come forward and put your feet on the necks of these kings." So, they came forward and put their feet on their necks. Then Joshua said to them, "Never fear or be dismayed. Chazak! Be strong! For thus will ADONAI do to all your enemies whom you will fight. (Joshua 10:24–25)

Joshua gave this visual representation of what God was going to do to all of their enemies. Basically, he was telling them that they were the head and not the tail. They were above their enemies and not beneath them. He told them to be strong. Don't ever forget who your God is, and remember, the battle belongs to the Lord.

Nearing the Finish Line

The long saga of Israel's conquest of the Promised Land was coming to a close. Our scene opens up with yet another king hearing of the exploits of God and gathering an alliance of forces to fight Israel.

Previously on our journey with Joshua, Adoni-zedek, king of Jerusalem, heard of the defeat of Ai and the surrender of Gibeon. Upon hearing this news, he enlisted the help of four other Amorite kings and their armies. Leaving their cities, these four kings, along with their armies, joined the king of Jerusalem and laid siege to the city of Gibeon.

Israel heard of the siege and came to the aid of Gibeon, making it five armies against one. Not very good odds when looking in the natural, but when you add God to the equation—any equation for that matter—the odds always fall in his favor.

These five kings from the south were utterly and completely defeated by ADONAI-Tzva'ot. In fact, Scripture specifically tells us that it was ADONAI who threw them into confusion. It was ADONAI who defeated these five armies with a crushing defeat. It was also ADONAI who chased them down the road, all the while hurling great stones from heaven, taking them out one by one. Scripture tells us that more of them died by those hailstones than by the sword of Israel. This was God's battle, and this was his victory.

The southern portion of Canaan now laid under the control of Israel. Here in this passage, we see the kings of the north being stirred up by Jabin, king of Hazor, who was the lead king, if you will, of northern Canaan.

> Now when Jabin king of Hazor heard about it, he
> sent word to Jobab king of Madon, to the king

of Shimron, to the king of Achshaph, and to the
kings in the north, in the hill country, in the
Arabah south of Chinneroth, in the lowland and
in the regions of Dor to the west, the Canaanites
in the east and west, the Amorites, the Hittites,
the Perizzites, the Jebusites in the hill country
and the Hivites at the foot of Hermon in the land
of Mizpah. So, they came out, they and all their
armies with them, a multitude with as many
people as the sand on the seashore, with very
many horses and chariots. All these kings joined
forces, came and camped together at the waters
of Merom to fight with Israel. (Joshua 11:1–5)

Hazor undoubtedly was the largest most influential city in all
of Canaan. Its size was huge, two hundred acres, with an estimated
population of thirty thousand. It was ideally situated for economic
and political dominance, and Jabin was its king. Like Adoni-zedek,
Jabin rallied other kings who presumably owed him their allegiance,
dispatching messengers to King Jobab of Madon, the unnamed kings
of Shimrom and Achshaph, as well as to the other unnamed kings of
the north. However, he didn't stop there. He also sent messengers to
the east and west, which included the Amorites, Hittites, Perizzites,
Jebusites as well as the Hivites at the foot of Hermon in the land of
Mizpah.

This army was exceptional, like nothing Israel had seen before,
even in the early days when they battled the Amalekites or when
they fought against the Amorite kings Og and Sihon. All that paled
in comparison to the army that was now coming out against Israel.

This army was huge in number. In fact, Josephus, the Jewish
secular historian, tells us that Jabin amassed a marching army of
approximately three hundred thousand soldiers. That didn't include
the ten thousand horsemen or the twenty thousand chariots that
accompanied those foot soldiers.[35]

Joshua 11:4 describes this massive army as having "many people
as the sand on the seashore." It also speaks of many horses and char-

iots. Now the chariots in those days were like tanks, iron tipped and manufactured to rip through the formed lines of the enemy, an ominous note for poor Israel, who would be facing this enemy on foot.

The first five verses in Joshua, chapter 11, create the impression that everyone had come from everywhere and with frightening firepower. The biggest battle was about to begin. Then comes verse 6 which starts off with "But ADONAI."

I want to pause here and bring attention to a phrase that will become our next life lesson, and that is this: "*But God…*" This phrase interrupts the devil's plan for your life.

The enemy brings destruction, *but God* brings life. The enemy declares war, *but God* declares victory. The enemy brings fear, *but God* brings hope.

> But ADONAI said to Joshua, "Do not be afraid because of them, for tomorrow at this time I will give all of them slain before Israel. You are to hamstring their horses and burn their chariots with fire. (Joshua 11:6)

Once again, we see God giving a word of assurance and then a promise, immediately followed by a word of instruction.

- You don't have to fear them.
- Keep your eyes on me.
- By this time tomorrow, I will hand them over to you.
- All of them, *dead.*
- Now this is what you are to do.

Once more, we see God giving instruction to Joshua on how to fight the enemy. You will find that with each new adversary, Joshua received specific instructions on how to defeat the enemy he was facing.

With the Amalekites, it was by lifting up the rod of God, a representation of both his presence and his authority. With Og and Sihon, it was a frontal attack with the sword.

It was at Jericho that God introduced them to the art of psychological warfare as they marched around the city, continually blowing the shofarot.

At Ai, God showed them the method of the sneak attack through multiple ambushes. With Gibeon, they defeated the kings of the south by God's supernatural intervention—God moving through their ranks with a deafening noise, throwing them into utter confusion. He then chased them while hurling hailstones at them, crushing them with a crushing defeat, climaxing with both the sun and moon standing still, extending the day another twenty-four hours—a supernatural victory.

God's plan of attack against this massive army would be the element of surprise. Joshua and the army of Israel had been instructed to hamstring the horses and set the chariots on fire.

Let's pause here for just a moment and imagine this scene as it unfolds. A multitude of soldiers, more than the sand of the sea, had gathered together in one place. They had camped at the waters of Merom in preparation of attacking Joshua and the army of Israel.

Word got to Joshua about this massive army that had come out against them. Notice that he didn't wait for them to attack Israel. He went on the offense. Simply upon hearing the promises of God, Joshua set out.

God revealed to them where this army was camped, and they entered into enemy territory by stealth. Upon God's instructions, they were to hamstring the horses and set the chariots on fire.

The word *hamstring* comes from the Hebrew word *aw-kar*. This word describes the method of crippling a person or animal so that they cannot walk properly by severing the hamstring tendons in the thigh.[36] And that's exactly what the army of Israel began to do.

Quietly and systematically, they began positioning themselves by the horses and chariots. They would need to disable approximately thirty thousand horses. Remember, there were ten thousand horsemen; however, we also have to keep in mind that there were twenty thousand chariots that were drawn by horses as well. So there were approximately thirty thousand horses that had to be taken out of commission simultaneously.

At the exact same time they were hamstringing the horses, they had to simultaneously set fire to twenty thousand chariots. Keep in mind that there were approximately forty thousand soldiers within the armed forces of Israel. So this sneak attack would need precision and accuracy.

In order to keep the element of surprise, Israel would need to position themselves one soldier per horse (30,000) while the remaining soldiers (10,000) were prepping the chariots to be lit.

When the chariots were all prepped for burning, ten thousand Israeli soldiers would have the responsibility of lighting up twenty thousand chariots at the same time the remaining soldiers cut the hamstrings.

The unsuspecting soldiers of Jabin's army were in for a rude awakening. The silence of the night was suddenly shattered. Slumbering soldiers were quickly awakened by neighing horses and chariots afire. Utter chaos and confusion swept through the enemy's camp as the armed forces of Israel attacked. Once again, God had taken the enemy by surprise.

> So, Joshua and all the people of war with him attacked them suddenly at the waters of Merom and fell upon them. Then ADONAI gave them into the hand of Israel, so they defeated them and chased them as far as Great Zidon and Misrephoth-maim, and up to the Valley of Mizpeh eastward. They struck them down until they left no survivors. Joshua did to them as ADONAI had instructed him—he hamstrung their horses and burnt their chariots with fire. (Joshua 11:7–9)

Our next Life Lesson is a vital truth that we need to keep in the forefront of our mind, and that is this: *victory is not achieved on the battlefield but, rather, in the preparation.*

The time to sharpen your sword isn't when you hear the sounding of the shofar. That's the time to unsheathe your sword, not sharpen it.

I have treasured Your word in my heart, so I
might not sin against you. (Psalm 119:11)

Some translations will use the word *hid* in place of the word *treasured*. However, the word *treasured* speaks not only about something that is of great value, but it also speaks of hiding that of great value so that it cannot be taken from you.

We are to treasure and hide God's word in our hearts so that we don't sin against him. Oftentimes, we associate sin with doing things that are displeasing to God, things such as lying, stealing, gossiping, etc. However, in Paul's letter to the believers in Rome, he writes that "whatever is not of faith, is sin."[37]

Faith is a simple trust and an absolute confidence in God. That trust, that confidence comes through hearing, studying, and obeying God's word.

I treasure God's word and hide it inside of me so that I would not doubt his love, ability, or his character. I treasure his word so that my trust in him is not hindered by my circumstances.

We are to study God's word, putting it into our heart so that when the enemy comes with the voice of temptation, we will know exactly how to answer him.

The Amplified Bible translates Proverbs 15:28 in this way, "The mind of the uncompromisingly righteous studies how to answer." The application of this scripture is the implementation of the Life Lesson: *But God*, the phrase that attests to the interruption of the enemy's plans for your life.

The writer of Hebrews describes God's word as being a two-edged sword, and Paul describes God's word as being the sword that the Spirit wields.[38] The midst of the battle isn't the time to either sharpen your sword or look for your sword. Being prepared is being ready for whatever comes your way. This is the application of the Life

Lesson: *whatever comes at me, I am safe because he is my covering.* God is my shield; he is my body armor.

Throughout this time, Joshua had learned the importance of having a continual conversation with God, of taking those selah moments and seeking God's counsel, his direction, and his plans.

> Just as ADONAI had commanded Moses His servant, so Moses commanded Joshua, and so Joshua did. He left nothing undone of all that ADONAI had commanded Moses. (Joshua 11:15)

Joshua didn't stop. He didn't relent. He didn't slow down. He didn't weary in the task. He continually drew his strength from God. Joshua didn't rely upon his own strength, his own insight, or wit. He learned to trust God and to look to him for direction.

> So, Joshua captured all this land: the hill country, the Negev, all the land of Goshen, the lowland, the Arabah, the hill country of Israel and its lowland, from the Mount Halak that ascends to Seir all the way to Baal-gad in the valley of Lebanon at the foot of Mount Hermon. He captured all their kings, struck down and put them to death. For a long time, Joshua made war with all those kings. (Joshua 11:16–18)

Joshua finished what he started. Not only did Joshua learn from his mistakes, but he learned through his victories as well. God is righteous. God is just. God is faithful.

As we continue with this passage of Scripture, I want to draw your attention to the next two verses here in Joshua, chapter 11, verses that give us a small glimpse into the plans and purposes of God.

> There was not a city that made peace with Bnei-Yisrael except the Hivites who inhabited Gibeon. All the rest they took in battle. For it

was of ADONAI to harden their hearts to encounter Israel in battle, that they might be put to the
ban, that they might receive no mercy, in order to
destroy them as ADONAI had commanded Moses.
(Joshua 11:19–20)

For just a moment, I want us to revisit those enlisted in the
army of Jabin who lived in the land of Mizpah.

The Canaanites in the east and west, the Amorites,
the Hittites, the Perizzites, the Jebusites in the hill
country and the Hivites at the foot of Hermon in
the land of Mizpah. (Joshua 11:3)

The Gibeonites were Hivites who had aligned themselves with
Israel. They chose the side of righteousness. They chose to cross
lines and stand alongside the children of Israel as they followed
the Commander of heaven's armies. That means they were fighting
against their own during the battle with Jabin.

More often than not, we have looked at this treaty between the
Gibeonites and Israel as one of deception—Israel being tricked into
aligning themselves with the enemy. Yes, Israel was deceived, and
yes, they made their decision based upon their circumstances. Yet
through Scripture, we see God's hand in that alliance.

It was ADONAI who softened the hearts of the Gibeonites. It was
ADONAI who drew them to his heart. They heard his voice, responded
to his leading, and they put their trust in him. Yeshua explains this
very process in the Gospel of John.

Everyone the Father gives Me will come to Me,
and anyone coming to Me I will never reject.
(John 6:37)

No one can come to Me unless My Father who
sent Me draws Him. (John 6:44)

> Amen, amen I tell you, whoever hears My word
> and trusts the One who sent Me has eternal life.
> He does not come into judgment, but has passed
> over from death to life. (John 5:24)

The Gibeonites didn't come to Israel on their own accord. They were drawn by God. They responded to that drawing the only way they knew how. They came wrapped in deception, but God saw right through their disguise to the heart of the matter.

> So they replied to him: "Your servants have come
> from a very distant country because of the Name
> of Adonai your God." (Joshua 9:9)

We now know that if Joshua had had a conversation with God prior to making their decision, they would not have been deceived. God would have revealed to them exactly who the Gibeonites were and that he had drawn them to Israel. They were deceived. God was not.

> I know You can do all things; no purpose of Yours
> can be thwarted. (Job 42:2)

God spared Rahab and Gibeon not because of what they had done but because it was in his heart to do so. God chose them. He hand selected them to be his instruments, fulfilling his plans and his purposes.

> You did not choose Me, but I chose you. I selected
> you so that you would go and produce fruit, and
> your fruit would remain. (John 15:16)

God chose Joshua, and he chose Rahab. He chose Gibeon, and he has chosen you.

The Art of Application
and Impartation

Life Lessons & selah moments—during this journey, we have been taking an in-depth look at the sanctified experiences throughout the leadership of Joshua. Through these experiences, we have gleaned several Life Lessons. If we are faithful to apply these lessons to our lives on a daily basis, we will undergo that inner transformation that God so desires in each and every one of our lives.

However, it's not enough to simply read these Life Lessons or to even learn them if we are not going to apply them to our lives.

God's word to Joshua was to meditate upon his words. Just as God told Moses to rehearse these words to Joshua, we are to rehearse the righteous rulings of our God day and night, night and day.

> This book of the Torah should not depart from your mouth—you are to meditate on it day and night, so that you may be careful to do everything written in it. For then you will make your ways prosperous and then you will be successful. (Joshua 1:8)

We've learned that the word *meditate* means more than just focusing your thoughts on something. It does mean that, but it takes it one step further in that you are to utter, speak, and rehearse that which you are focusing upon.

We are to fix our minds on God's word, his Torah, and we are to focus our thoughts on what he says. We are then instructed to repeat or rehearse the righteous sayings of our God. We are to hear, and we are to do.

However, it doesn't stop with the application of these principles either. God's desire is not only for us to learn and apply them to our lives but to also impart them to others. It is the art of application and impartation that God wants to perfect in our lives.

So before this journey comes to an end, we are going to revisit each of these Life Lessons. We are going to take a selah moment. We are going to *stop*, *look*, and *listen*. In so doing, we're going to take a closer look at these Life Lessons through the lens of our own personal lives, asking ourselves the question "How do these truths relate to me personally?"

We are going to do this through what I like to refer to as the SOAP process, a method of studying, applying, and imparting.

Every one of us has something that someone else needs. In essence, you and I are God's answer to someone else's prayer. Paul speaks of this very thing in his opening remarks to the believers in Rome.

> For I long to see you, so I may share with you [*or impart to you*] some spiritual gift to strengthen you. That is to say, we would be encouraged together by one another's faithfulness—both yours and mine. (Romans 1:11–12)

The word SOAP is an acronym that means the following:

- S Scripture (or, in this case, Life Lesson)
- O Observation (What truth are you seeing within these words?)
- A Application (How can you apply this to your life, thus, ushering in the necessary change that will bring about inner transformation?)
- P Prayer (having a conversation with God on how you can then impart this truth to someone else)

The art of application and impartation is so that we truly can be *talmadim* making talmadim—disciples making disciples. These are the Life Lessons that we have learned throughout our journey with Joshua. Using the SOAP method (*S*cripture/Life Lesson, *O*bservation, *A*pplication, *P*rayer for applying and imparting), read and review each lesson and then write what you have observed through your personal lens. Write down the application for your life and then your prayer for applying and imparting that truth.

1. With each and every change, there is always a promise and a word of instruction. (Joshua 1:3–5)

    _____
    _____
    _____
    _____
    _____
    _____

2. You are not defined by your past, nor your present circumstances. Your identity, your worth is wrapped up in the very essence of who God is and how he sees you. (Joshua 2:1–2)

    _____
    _____
    _____
    _____
    _____
    _____

3. Experiences are meant for remembering, not repeating. (Joshua 3:1–5)

    _____
    _____
    _____
    _____
    _____
    _____

4. Our attention isn't to be focused on the *method* but, rather, the Master. (Joshua 3:6–13)

_____

_____

_____

_____

_____

_____

5. It has to be his will, his way, *always.* (Joshua 4:8–9, 18–20)

_____

_____

_____

_____

_____

6. It was ADONAI. It has always been ADONAI. It will always be ADONAI. (Joshua 5:4–7)

_____

_____

_____

_____

_____

7. Even when our own eyes can't see, God is there. He is always right there. (Joshua 5:13)

_____

_____

_____

_____

_____

8. God never chooses sides as he is always on the side of *righteousness*. (Joshua 5:14–15)

_____

_____

_____

_____

_____

_____

9. You are to see this *fight* from the *victory* and proceed accordingly. (Joshua 6:1)

_____

_____

_____

_____

_____

10. Earnestly wait for his plans to develop regarding you. (Joshua 6:22–25)

_____

_____

_____

_____

_____

11. Trust him. He will do it. (Joshua 6:22–25)

_____

_____

_____

_____

_____

12. God should always be your *go-to* person. (Joshua 7:6–9)

_____

_____

_____

_____

_____

_____

13. It's not about you. Stop and look at the bigger picture. (Joshua 7:8–9)

_____

_____

_____

_____

_____

_____

14. Sin is like a landmine. It affects everyone around you. (Joshua 7:1)

_____

_____

_____

_____

_____

15. Don't stop asking. Don't stop seeking. (Joshua 7:1–2)

_____

_____

_____

_____

_____

LIFE LESSONS & SELAH MOMENTS

16. Whatever has your focus has you. (Joshua 7:21)

_____
_____
_____
_____
_____
_____

17. The acknowledgment of sin is not equivalent to the repentance of sin. (Joshua 7:22–24)

_____
_____
_____
_____
_____
_____

18. Learn the importance of taking a selah moment. (Joshua 9:3–14)

_____
_____
_____
_____
_____
_____

19. Don't miss an opportunity to hear God speak. (Joshua 9:14)

_____
_____
_____
_____
_____
_____

147

20. God always has the last word, but it's up to you whether that word will be one of judgment or mercy. (Joshua 9:24)

_____

_____

_____

_____

_____

_____

21. If you want God to open his mouth, then you must open his Word. (Joshua 10:6–7)

_____

_____

_____

_____

_____

22. God is your covering. Whatever comes at you, you are safely hidden under his wings. (Joshua 10:10–11)

_____

_____

_____

_____

_____

23. Now is a good time to talk with God. (Joshua 10:11–12)

_____

_____

_____

_____

_____

24. But God—this phrase interrupts the devil's plan for your life. (Joshua 11:6)

_____

_____

_____

_____

_____

_____

25. Victory is not achieved on the battlefield but, rather, in the preparation. (Joshua 11:7–14)

_____

_____

_____

_____

_____

_____

Glossary of Terms

ADONAI. Hebrew for "LORD." When written in small capitals, it refers to God's personal name YHWH as given in the Hebrew Bible. This personal name is God's "covenant name," used when God is relating to the Jewish people in an intimate way. Since its pronunciation is not known, and also out of respect for God's name, Jews traditionally substitute the word ADONAI. (Exodus 3:15; Jeremiah 1:9; Psalm 1:2; Matthew 1:22; Mark 5:19; Luke 1:5; John 1:23)

ADONAI Elohim. Hebrew for "LORD God." This title links Israel's God, the God of the Covenant, with God as creator of the Universe. (Genesis 2:4; Isaiah 48:16; Psalm 72:18; Luke 1:32; Revelation 1:8)

ADONAI-Nissi. Hebrew for the "LORD our banner." (Exodus 17:15; Psalm 20:1)

ADONAI Elohei-Tzva'ot. Hebrew for "LORD God of Hosts" or "LORD God of [heaven's] Armies." The Greek equivalent is *Kurios o Theos o Pantokrator*, which is literally "LORD God Almighty" or "LORD God, Ruler over All." (Jeremiah 15:16; Psalm 89:9; Revelation 4:8; 21:22)

ADONAI-TZVA'OT. Hebrew for "LORD of Hosts" or "LORD of [heaven's] Armies." The Greek equivalent is *Kurios Sabaoth* (Isaiah 6:3), but the Septuagint often translates this Hebrew title as *Kurios Pantokrator*, which is literally "LORD Almighty" or "LORD, Ruler over All" (2 Samuel 7:8)

Bnei-Yisrael. Literally, "the sons of Israel" or "the children of Israel," this term is used frequently in the *Tanakh* (*see Tanahk*) to represent the entire Jewish nation. (Exodus 1:17; Joshua 3:9; Nehemiah 1:6; Romans 9:27; Revelation 7:4)

Chazak. Hebrew for "be strong!" Often used as a command of encouragement and rally. The phrase "Chazak, chazak, v'nit chazek!" (Be strong, be strong, and be strengthened!") is repeated after the completed reading of each book of the Torah (*see Torah*) throughout the yearly Jewish reading cycle. (Deuteronomy 31:6; Joshua 1:9; Nahum 2:2; Psalm 31:25)

Elyon. A title for God, meaning "Most High." (Luke 1:35, 7–6; Acts 7:48) A longer form is *El Elyon*, "God Most High." (Deuteronomy 32:8; Isaiah 14:14; Psalm 91:1; Acts 16:17)

Emissaries. Hebrew for "apostles" or "messengers."

Hineni. Hebrew for "Here I am." It is mostly used when God personally calls on someone in the Bible to do something difficult and important. (Genesis 22:1; Exodus 3:4)

Kohanim. Hebrew for "priests." It is the plural derivative of the word *kohen* meaning "priest." (Joshua 4:3; 2 Peter 2:9; Revelation 1:6)

Matzah. Plural form is *matzot,* unleavened bread which is made without yeast, eaten especially during the feast of Passover. (Exodus 13:6; Leviticus 2:3; Matthew 26:17; Mark 14:22)

Messiah. A title meaning "Anointed One," often used in speaking of a redeemer sent from God to free his people from exile and oppression. The Greek equivalent is "Christ." (Matthew 1:16; Mark 8:29; Luke 2:11; John 1:41)

Mitzvot. Plural form of *mitzvah*, a commandment from God. (Deuteronomy 11:22; 2 Kings 17:37; Proverbs 6:20)

Pesach. Hebrew word for "Passover," used also for the Passover lamb whose blood on the door caused the angel of death to "pass over" the Israelite home in Egypt. *Yeshua (see Yeshua)* is called the Passover Lamb because his blood saves individuals from sin and death. (Leviticus 23:4; Numbers 28:16; Luke 2:41; John 18:1 title)

Ruach ha-Kodesh. The Hebrew name for the Holy Spirit, the Spirit of God. (Isaiah 63:11; Psalms 51:13; Matthew 28:19)

Shaddai. A common name for God in the *Tanach*, (*see Tanach*) usually translated as "Almighty." The name is often used in a combination such as *El Shaddai*, "God Almighty." (Genesis 17:1; Ezekiel 1:24; Job 11:7)

Shalom. The Hebrew word for "peace." It also can mean "wholeness" or "well-being." Shalom is often used as a greeting (hello) or as a farewell (goodbye). (Genesis 26:31; 1 Samuel 16:4; Matthew 10:13; Mark 9:50; John 14:27)

Shofar. A ram's horn used in the Bible for summoning armies, calling to repentance, and in other situations. Blasts of various lengths and numbers signified different instructions. Plural form is *shofarot*. (Joshua 6:4–5)

Sukkah. Hebrew word for "tabernacle." A temporary dwelling, such as the booths constructed during the Feast of *Sukkot* (Tabernacles.) It is also used in the *Tanakh (see Tanakh)* of the tent in which God dwelt among the Jewish people, both in the wilderness and in the land of Israel.

Talmadim. Plural form of *Talmid.* Hebrew word for "disciple." (Matthew 28:19; John 1:35)

Tanakh. The Hebrew Scriptures. Commonly referred to as the "Old Testament."

Torah. Literally "instruction," this term can refer to the five books of Moses or more generally to God's commandments.

Yeshua. The Hebrew name of our Messiah, known in English as "Jesus." The name means "salvation." (Matthew 1:21; Mark 6:14; Luke 2:21; John 19:19)

Notes

Endnotes

1 *Strong's Exhaustive Concordance*, Bible Study Tools. Accessed April 10, 2020. http:/www.biblestudytools.com/lexicons/Hebrew/kjv/suwm.html.

2 *Strong's Exhaustive Concordance*, Bible Study Tools. Accessed April 11, 2020. http:/www.biblestudytools.com/lexicons/Hebrew/kjv/chazaq.html.

3 Merriam Webster Incorporated, *Merriam Webster Online Dictionary*. Last modified June 11, 2011. Accessed April 11, 2020. http://www.merriam-webster.com/dictionary/resolute.

4 Merriam Webster Incorporated, *Merriam Webster Online Dictionary*. Last modified June 11, 2011. Accessed April 11, 2020. http://www.merriam-webster.com/dictionary/observe.

5 *Strong's Exhaustive Concordance*, Bible Study Tools. Accessed April 11, 2020. http:/www.biblestudytools.com/lexicons/Hebrew/kjv/yare.html.

6 *Strong's Exhaustive Concordance*, Bible Study Tools. Accessed April 11, 2020. http:/www.biblestudytools.com/lexicons/Hebrew/kjv/hagah.html.

7 Merriam Webster Incorporated, *Merriam Webster Online Dictionary*. Last modified June 11, 2011. Accessed April 12, 2020. http://www.merriam-webster.com/dictionary/spy.

8 Matthew 1:1–6

9 *Strong's Exhaustive Concordance*, Bible Study Tools. Accessed April 18, 2020. http:/www.biblestudytools.com/lexicons/Hebrew/kjv/yar-dane.html.

10 *Strong's Exhaustive Concordance*, Bible Study Tools. Accessed April 18, 2020. http:/www.biblestudytools.com/lexicons/Hebrew/kjv/gilgal.html.

11   Esther 3:7

12   Genesis 17:7–11

13   *Strong's Exhaustive Concordance*, Bible Study Tools. Accessed April 19, 2020. http:/www.biblestudytools.com/lexicons/Hebrew/kjv/cherpah.html.

14   *Strong's Exhaustive Concordance*, Bible Study Tools. Accessed April 25, 2020. http:/www.biblestudytools.com/lexicons/Hebrew/kjv/amats.html.

15   Isaiah 9:5 TLV (verse 6 in other translations)

16   *Strong's Exhaustive Concordance*, Bible Study Tools. Accessed April 25, 2020. http:/www.biblestudytools.com/lexicons/Hebrew/kjv/gibbor.html.

17   *Strong's Exhaustive Concordance*, Bible Study Tools. Accessed April 25, 2020. http:/www.biblestudytools.com/lexicons/Hebrew/kjv/ra'ah.html.

18   Merriam Webster Incorporated, *Merriam Webster Online Dictionary*. Last modified June 11, 2011. Accessed April 25, 2020. http://www.merriam-webster.com/dictionary/march.

19   Joshua 1:3

20   1 Corinthians 3:9

21   *Strong's Exhaustive Concordance*, Bible Study Tools. Accessed April 26, 2020. http:/www.biblestudytools.com/lexicons/Hebrew/kjv/herem.html.

22   *Strong's Exhaustive Concordance*, Bible Study Tools. Accessed April 25, 2020. http:/www.biblestudytools.com/lexicons/Hebrew/kjv/ma'hal.html.

23   *Strong's Exhaustive Concordance*, Bible Study Tools. Accessed April 26, 2020. http:/www.biblestudytools.com/lexicons/Hebrew/kjv/ra'ah.html.

24   Merriam Webster Incorporated, *Merriam Webster Online Dictionary*. Last modified June 11, 2011. Accessed April 26, 2020. http://www.merriam-webster.com/dictionary/covet.

25   Genesis 10:10; Genesis 11:2; Genesis 14:1; Genesis 14:9; Joshua 7:21; Isaiah 11:11; Daniel 1:2; Zechariah 5:11

26   *Strong's Exhaustive Concordance*, Bible Study Tools. Accessed April 26, 2020. http:/www.biblestudytools.com/lexicons/Hebrew/kjv/addereth.html.

27   Proverbs 15:27a

28   *Strong's Exhaustive Concordance*, Bible Study Tools. Accessed May 2, 2020. http:/www.biblestudytools.com/lexicons/Hebrew/kjv/achor.html.

29   *Strong's Exhaustive Concordance*, Bible Study Tools. Accessed May 2, 2020. http:/www.biblestudytools.com/lexicons/Hebrew/kjv/kiydown.html.

30   Genesis 12:7–8

31   Deuteronomy 20:11

32   Joshua 5:13

33   *Strong's Exhaustive Concordance*, Bible Study Tools. Accessed May 3, 2020. http:/www.biblestudytools.com/lexicons/Hebrew/kjv/hamam.html.

34   Merriam Webster Incorporated, *Merriam Webster Online Dictionary*. Last modified June 11, 2011. Accessed May 3, 2020. http://www.merriam-webster.com/dictionaryconfuse.

35   https://penelope.uchicago.edu/josephus/ant-5.html

36   *Strong's Exhaustive Concordance*, Bible Study Tools. Accessed May 16, 2020. http:/www.biblestudytools.com/lexicons/Hebrew/kjv/aw-kar.html.

37   Romans 14:23b

38   Hebrews 4:12; Ephesians 6:17

About the Author

Author, pastor, speaker Michelle M. Woodruff, ordained since 1989, has an extensive ministry background which enables her to reach others with humor, warmth, transparency, and strength. Her unique style of teaching is rich and profound, yet simple and easy to understand. With beautiful simplicity, she bridges the gap between Jewish and non-Jewish believers in Yeshua (*Jesus*), helping them to rediscover the Jewish roots of their Christian faith. Mother, grandmother, author, teacher, conference speaker, role model and mentor, Pastor Michelle is committed to building God's kingdom and seeing every believer become a true disciple of Messiah Yeshua (*Jesus Christ.*)

Michelle has authored other books on the Christian walk, in addition to the one you hold in your hand: *Exposure—Developing and Reflecting God's Image; Armed & Victorious—An In-Depth Study of the Armor of God; He Came to Set the Captives Free; and MJP—Make Jesus Proud.*

Michelle has three children and three grandchildren and lives in the Phoenix area. You can find her on Facebook @michellemwoodruff and correspond with her by email at mwoodruff47@gmail.com.

CPSIA information can be obtained
at www.ICGtesting.com
Printed in the USA
BVHW071050240321
603322BV00001B/199